Mills & Boon Classics

A chance to read and collect some of the best-loved novels from Mills & Boon – the world's largest publisher of romantic fiction.

Every month, four titles by favourite Mills & Boon authors will be re-published in the *Classics* series.

A list of other titles in the *Classics* series can be found at the end of this book.

ꝯP

Anne Mather

SEEN BY CANDLELIGHT

MILLS & BOON LIMITED
LONDON · TORONTO

First published 1966 under the title
Design for Loving
Philippine copyright 1977
This edition 1977

ISBN 0 263 72507 3

Set in 10 on 11pt Baskerville

Made and Printed in Great Britain by
C. Nicholls & Company Ltd
The Philips Park Press, Manchester

"Yes," I answered you last night;
"No," this morning, sir, I say.
Colours seen by candlelight
Will not look the same by day.

Elizabeth Barrett Browning, *The Lady's Yes*

CHAPTER ONE

KAREN STACEY slid out of the driving seat of her small black saloon and slipped her sheepskin overcoat about her shoulders before locking the car door. Shivering slightly in the frosty March air, she crossed the pavement and opened the door of the Georgian-styled cottage which her mother owned in this quiet mews.

Inside all was warmth and light and Karen shrugged appreciatively in the pleasant atmosphere. Liza, her mother's housekeeper, greeted her warmly, taking her coat and hanging it in the hall closet. Liza had been with her mother since Karen was a child, and yet to Karen, she never seemed to look any older.

With a smile now, Karen asked: "Where is my mother, Liza?"

"In the sitting-room, Miss Karen," replied Liza, her eyes showing their dislike of Karen's casual attire. Tight-fitting stretch slacks and a chunky sweater were anathema to Liza. "Must you wear those disgusting trousers, love?" she exclaimed. "They're hardly suitable for a young lady."

Liza was terribly old-fashioned. She had never married herself and had always looked on the Stacey children as her own. And with the familiarity of years she invariably spoke her mind. It amused Karen now and she answered:

"Oh, Liza darling, I've just left my drawing-board. You can't possibly expect me to dress up just to come round here. Not when I've got to go back and go on working. Besides, slacks are very warm and very fashionable at the moment."

Liza shrugged, grimacing, and with a chuckle Karen left her to enter the sitting-room. This was the room which overlooked Masewood Mews and was a very pleasant room. The whole cottage was comfortably, if not opulently furnished, and Mrs. Stacey lived here with her younger daughter, Sandra. Karen did not see as much of them as she should, she knew, but her work and the painting she did in her spare time kept her quite busy and besides, this house brought back too many painful memories which were best forgotten.

Her mother was seated at a bureau writing letters when Karen entered the room and she rose to greet her elder daughter. There was little resemblance between them, for Karen was an ash-blonde while her mother's hair had once been a vivid auburn.

Mrs. Stacey crossed the room and bestowed a kiss on her daughter's cold cheek. Then she drew back and surveyed her thoroughly.

"It's good to see you," said Karen, smiling. "It's so long since I've done so."

"Yes, darling," murmured Madeline Stacey absently. "I . . . er . . . I didn't hear you arrive."

"From your tone on the telephone I assumed a major catastrophe was about to occur," remarked Karen lightly. "I had visions of your waiting on the doorstep for my arrival. Instead, you seem engrossed with your own thoughts."

Madeline sighed heavily. "Well, my dear, I must admit I am rather cross with you for neglecting us for so long. We are your only kith and kin, you know. You really ought to care about us."

"But I do," exclaimed Karen, guiltily aware of her own indiscretions. "It's simply that I never seem to have the time. I lead a very full life really, Mother. But anyway, what is there to stop you from visiting me? The apartment is only a stone's throw away."

Madeline raised her eyebrows. "My dear Karen, whenever I visit you I find myself thrust to one side like so much rubbish, while you engross yourself in some new design or paint those ghastly abstracts. Alternatively, I'm entertained, but am always conscious that I'm stopping you from getting on. I could hardly say I was made welcome, however unkind that may sound."

Karen felt uncomfortable. She knew that what her mother had said was partly true, but Madeline's limited conversation, which was mainly gossip anyway, bored her stiff, and she did prefer to work alone.

"All right, honey," she agreed now. "You've made your point quite thoroughly. Now, what's your problem? The one that's hot off the press?"

Madeline indicated that Karen should sit down on a low armchair and turned away slowly. Karen sighed in exasperation. Much as she really loved her mother she knew only too well how she adored to dramatize things and it was obvious that this was not going to be the brief visit that she had hoped for. Madeline had something on her mind and she would not rest until she had extracted the very utmost out of it. Karen drew out her cigarette-case and helped herself to a cigarette, but her mother's first words startled her so much that she almost dropped it.

"Have you seen Paul lately?" began Madeline, in a contrivedly casual tone.

"Paul?" Karen felt as though she was playing for time. Time to gather her suddenly shocked senses together. With trembling fingers she lit the cigarette and inhaled deeply, savouring the nicotine in her lungs, relaxing. "No," she replied slowly. "We never meet, and you know it. Why do you ask? Oh . . . I suppose you saw the notice of his engagement in *The Times*."

"Yes, I did see that," agreed her mother slowly. "Ruth Delaney, I believe that was her name. Some American girl, a tycoon's daughter, if I remember correctly."

"You're in complete possession of the facts," remarked Karen rather dryly. This was no casual remark. "Well, Mother, why should I have seen Paul?"

Mrs. Stacey shrugged. "I thought perhaps he might have telephoned to object about Sandra going out with Simon."

Karen's eyes widened. "Simon!" she exclaimed. "Simon Frazer is going out with Sandra? But he's married; you must be joking."

"I only wish I were," said Madeline stiffly. "I don't joke about things like this, Karen. I'm at my wits' end. She refuses to give him up, even though I've begged her to do so. You know how unmanageable Sandra has always been, how headstrong and self-willed."

Karen frowned. "You have only yourself to blame for that," she said coolly. "You've always given in to her."

Madeline's lips thinned. "Thank you," she exclaimed furiously. "And what would you have done if you had been left alone with two young children to bring up?"

"I would have treated them both alike, instead of coddling one and making a rod for my own back," retorted Karen. "Anyway, Mother, that's hardly relevant now. I agree that Simon Frazer is no fit associate for any young girl, let alone an impressionable idiot like Sandra! How did you find out about them? I don't suppose she told you."

"Oh, no; not a word. A friend saw them dining together last week and couldn't wait to telephone me to let me know. Sandra is only seventeen, Karen. Simon Frazer must be over thirty; after all, Paul is thirty-seven, isn't he?"

"Ah, yes," Karen drew on her cigarette. "Where does Paul come into all this?" She shivered. "Simon is only his brother, you know."

"As I've already said, I asked Sandra to stop seeing Simon. She simply laughed at my arguments and refused to take any notice of me. She says she is perfectly capable of taking care of herself. Both you and I know how foolhardy that statement is with a man like him. Something has got to be done. I think Paul is the only person able to do that something."

"So?" Karen's voice was dangerously quiet.

"I want you to get in touch with Paul and ask him to speak to Simon – "

Karen sprang to her feet. "No!" she exclaimed abruptly. She ran a restless hand over her shoulder-length straight hair. "I won't do it. Paul and I parted in the divorce court two years ago and I just couldn't contact him now. It's out of the question."

Madeline frowned. "So your own pride is greater than your sister's downfall? She is your sister, Karen, your seventeen-year-old sister!"

"Stop play-acting, Mother," cried Karen, inwardly seething. "It won't work. I refuse to do it. Sandra is seventeen, as you've said. She's not a child. She must make her own mistakes. After all, I was only eighteen when I met Paul."

"And look what happened to your marriage," taunted her mother cruelly. "Five years and it was all over. Here you are, twenty-five years old and already a divorcee. Not that there's any question of marriage in the circumstances. As you've said, Simon is married. That makes everything so much worse."

Karen was pale. This conversation was raking up all the painful past that she had tried to bury these last two years. She had always known that her mother had resented her break with Paul for purely selfish reasons, but to fling it all in her face now almost brought Karen to tears. How could Madeline be so unkind? But tears were a luxury that Karen had never indulged in and she did not so so now. She had always been an independent sort of person, like her father, and Madeline had clung to the baby, Sandra, and spoiled her utterly when their father was killed in an air crash a long while ago.

Karen knew that Madeline wanted to save Sandra from herself and she did not care if she hurt her elder daughter in the process. Karen was tempted to leave immediately and let them work it out alone, but she knew if she did so, she would never be welcome here again. As her mother had said, she and Sandra were Karen's only blood relations and to cut herself off from them would leave her completely alone. How could she do such a thing?

"Well?" exclaimed her mother. "Are you going to let your sister's life be ruined?"

Karen sighed heavily. The ultimatum had come and she was not ready for it. What could she say? How could she explain that it was not merely pride that kept her from contacting Paul? That she was frightened of her treacherous emotions and afraid that he might see how disturbed she was.

But Simon, too, had a wife whom he never considered and although Karen had never liked Julia Frazer, she was still involved. Perhaps Paul might be glad to break up the affair. After all, he had no reason to love the Stacey family.

"All right," she agreed at last. "But why should you imagine that Paul will take any notice of me? Let alone speak to Simon."

"Paul used to be very fond of Sandra," replied Madeline, inwardly exulting at Karen's surrender. "And he knows what kind of a man Simon is."

Karen stubbed out her cigarette and thrust a hand into the pocket of her slacks. She was committed to speaking to her ex-husband. God, weren't memories hateful enough without reinforcing them with reality? How could you meet a man with whom you had shared the tenderest intimacies of marriage without feeling a knife turn in your inside? She supposed dully that it should have been easier, but they had been so much in love and now . . .

She had been eighteen when she met Paul Frazer. He was then the chairman of the board of the Frazer Textile Industries whose head office was in London, and Karen was a very junior designer working for the company. She had worked there for almost two years without ever dreaming she would come in contact with the young dynamic tycoon whose named spelled "Success" with a capital S. She had heard plenty about him from her colleagues, but he did not concern himself with the small fry like them. Still a bachelor at thirty, he was the most sought-after man in London, and the social papers and magazines splashed stories about him wherever he went.

For all this, Karen had secretly believed that the man could not seriously add up to his image. It had amused her to listen to the girls raving about him, but she had not been particularly interested. Men had always been attracted to her and she had plenty of admirers in her own sphere without looking on to a higher, much more futile, plane.

And then she produced, as much to her surprise as anybody else's, a design for a carpet which was quite brilliant. The Frazer Combine produced various ranges of textiles and the carpet design was a completely original piece of work.

To her embarrassment, she was sent for by the man himself, and had to go to his office on the sacrosanct top floor of the Frazer building. She had been not so much nervous as embarrassed, but when the chief designer introduced her to Paul Frazer she found herself completely absorbed by his overwhelming charm and personality. Far from over-estimating the man, she found him absolutely more devastating than his reputation and was therefore astonished when later in the week he rang her office and invited her to dinner.

She accepted, of course, much to the envy of her friends, and found to her amazement that he was actually interested in her as a person, and not as a designer.

Within a few weeks their relationship had assumed such proportions that Paul, who had never been used to being denied anything from a woman, found his every waking moment a torment of wanting to possess her, and his admiration for her ideals kindled into love. Karen, who had been attracted to him from the beginning fought against the love which threatened to overwhelm her, but when Paul eventually proposed marriage she was utterly consumed with happiness.

They had flown to the Bahamas for their honeymoon

and were away for three idyllic months. Karen had never known such happiness and Paul grew relaxed and lazy and sun-tanned. They adored each other, but when they returned to England to the house which Paul had bought near Richmond, they both resented the return to normality. Paul had to spend a lot of time at the office then, making up the work that had been left to slide in his absence, and Karen was left alone.

To begin with she was not lonely. The house needed a complete redecoration, and Paul had only a few of the rooms furnished so that Karen might do the whole place over to her own liking. With the help of a team of interior decorators Karen set to work, and the result pleased Paul just as much as Karen. She loved the evenings best when Paul came home to her. They rarely went out or entertained, and spent hours alone, talking and making love.

Then, as time passed, Paul, who had neglected a great deal of his normal work to be with Karen, found it necessary to visit the factories in the Midlands and the North of England where Frazer Textiles were produced. Being an active man, and interested in his work, he had always disliked delegating duty, and it was over a year since he had made a tour of inspection. With reluctance, he left Karen at home when he went to visit the factories. He knew if he took her with him he would be unable to concentrate. When she was with him nothing else could take precedence.

For a while, Karen's duties at Trevayne absorbed her, and she spent her time swimming in the pool in the grounds, or inviting friends over for tennis or drinks.

But as the years passed, apart from having holidays with Paul, their time together was limited to the evenings. Week-ends were given over to entertaining, and Karen began to hate the rigid pattern of their lives. She was bored; not with Paul but with having too much time and too little to do.

Eventually she asked Paul whether she could go back and work for the company. Paul was astounded, and refused point-blank. Apart from wanting her at home when he needed her, he objected to her working when it was so unnecessary. Her pleas of boredom were shrugged off, and Karen found herself getting irritable and frustrated. The combination of these two emotions began the series of arguments and rows about her work and about her aimless position in the house. Paul, who had assumed her too young to start a family, now suggested that they do just that, but Karen was too stubborn and foolish to agree and thus give in to him again. She refused abruptly, and to her horror Paul moved his clothes into the spare guest-room.

She was frightened and terrified of the results of her own actions, but too full of pride to beg him to come back to her.

They had been married a little over three years when Karen went behind Paul's back and got herself a job with a rival organization, the Martin Design Company. When Paul found out he was furious. The Martin Company obtained some of their work from the Frazer Syndicate, and he immediately withdrew his interest.

This culminated in yet another row, the result of which was that Karen packed her possessions and left. She had not gone to her mother's home. Her mother had never agreed that Karen should need anything more than a home and a husband, and she was very angry with Karen for a long time after their separation.

But for Karen there was no going back. Lewis Martin, the head of the small company, who knew her circumstances, sympathized with her but advised her to be brave and stick it out. He did not advise her to go back to Paul, indeed quite the reverse, and Karen was grateful to him at that time. Looking back now, she felt sure that left alone she would have returned to Paul within a week; and on his terms!

Paul made several abortive attempts to see her, but Lewis guarded her like the Crown Jewels and Karen was left alone with her thoughts. Whenever she suggested that perhaps she ought to see Paul, Lewis had reminded her of her reasons for leaving, and his words had stiffened her resolve. No good could come of their reunion. Only more arguments and more rows and another separation. They were incompatible. She might as well admit it here and now. Sexually, they were well matched, but marriages were only partly based on that side of things. These were Lewis's words, his advice to her, and she had believed him. After all, why not? He had nothing to gain in this except a rather second-rate designer who had forgotten so much during the past years. How was he to know that until the affair of the "Job" as she called it to herself, she and Paul had only rarely argued, and never in an unkind way?

Lewis found her the apartment which he obtained from a friend who was an estate agent. Lewis himself bought the flat and Karen was therefore his tenant. Karen was thrilled to have a home of her own and she furnished it as soon as she had saved the money. She did it in pieces, refusing Lewis's offer of an advance. Paul had long stopped calling her and she was left in peace. She worked well for Lewis, who was a good designer himself, and learned a lot from him.

He was a man in his early forties, a widower with no children, and Karen felt more like a daughter to him. It was with a sense of shock, therefore, that she received his proposal of marriage about a year after her break with Paul. She had protested that apart from the fact that she did not love him, she was technically still a married woman, and he had remarked that he had heard that Paul was going to sue her for divorce.

Karen was horrified a few days later when she received the notification in the mail of Paul's intention, and astounded that the grounds were adultery. He was citing Lewis as co-respondent.

Lewis however did not seem at all perturbed at his position in all this, even though the press made a nine days' wonder out of it all. He advised Karen not to defend the suit, as did the solicitor he found for her. Defended suits, they said, became laundries of dirty washing, and unless she wanted her private life dragged before the magistrate she might just as well not defend.

Bewildered, with no one to turn to but Lewis, Karen did as they suggested, and withdrew even more into her shell. Paul achieved his freedom by revealing certain facts which appeared conclusive to an outsider. Karen was too sick at heart to care. Of course Lewis had obtained the flat for her, but she paid a rent for it! Lewis often stayed late in the evening if they were discussing a new project, but it was all quite innocent. Even the night he had spent in the apartment on the couch in the living-room was only because a thick smog had descended on London, and it seemed ridiculous that Lewis should have to trail home to his house in Hampstead. However, even she could see that no good could come of trying to refute the accusations. They looked too conclusive, and Lewis's attitude was one of amiable inertia. Thus it was that less than five years after their wedding, Karen found herself free again.

Lewis was a tower of strength in those early days, devoting himself to her welfare and generally making himself indispensable. But when he again broached the subject of their marriage she vetoed the idea at once. Apart from anything else she felt too raw inside to contemplate such a step then, and Lewis, who knew he had no rivals, was content to wait.

Time had eventually partially healed Karen's torn feelings and she had thought she was beginning to get over the affair, but now, listening to her mother extolling Paul's virtues and ridiculing her own part in it, she knew that it was only pushed into the back of her mind, waiting to be brought into the open. And she felt convinced that all her futile defences were going to be in vain.

Still, she had committed herself and there was no going back now. She had to go through with it, see her ex-husband, for she could not discuss this over the telephone, and possibly even meet Ruth Delaney, the woman he had chosen to take her place.

Karen walked restlessly to the door. She might as well do it and get it over with.

"And ... er ... what if he refuses to even speak to me?" asked Karen, turning back to her mother.

"I'm sure he won't," replied Madeline calmly. "Paul isn't a man like that."

It had been a great blow to Madeline when she had had to give up giving her intimate little parties which Paul had indulged her in. He had always made sure she had plenty of money for anything she desired, and flowers and chocolates were often delivered for her. He had known all her little weaknesses, and even if a secretary carried out his instructions, Madeline revelled in the feeling of being a cosseted woman again. Karen had not known half of the money spent on Madeline, which was just as well, as she would have hated that Paul should think they were paupers.

"Well, why can't you ring him, then?" asked Karen, making one last attempt to free herself from her obligations.

"I couldn't, Karen. I wouldn't know what to say. You were his wife. You know him intimately. It will be much easier coming from you."

Karen flushed. Yes, she had known Paul intimately. She had thought that no one could possibly know anyone as she had known Paul.

"Now," said Madeline, smiling in her victory. "Will you ring him from here?" She glanced at her watch. "It's eleven-thirty. He may be at the office."

"No," replied Karen with emphasis. "I shall ring him from the intimacy of my own apartment. That is ... if you don't mind, of course." This last she spoke sarcastically, causing Madeline to press her lips together in a thin line.

"So long as you don't forget," she replied curtly.

"I shan't forget," replied Karen heavily. "I'll ring him when I get back. Does that satisfy you?"

"I imagine so," said Madeline coolly. "You'll have coffee before you go, won't you?"

Karen shook her head. The strained atmosphere was stifling her.

"No, thanks," she answered swiftly. "I . . . I'd better go. I have a lot to do."

"Of course," Madeline shrugged, and Karen went out into the hall to retrieve her coat. She felt nauseated and longed for the peace of her own home.

With a brief farewell, she slid behind the wheel of the Morris and drove round to Berkshire Court, the large block of apartments in a cul-de-sac in Chelsea, of which she occupied the top floor. It enabled her to have the maximum amount of light into the small studio which adjoined the flat and she had always liked it.

A lift transported her to the twelfth floor after she had put her car away in the basement garages. She walked along the corridor and inserted her key into the lock and entered the lounge of the apartment. This was an attractive room, with stark white walls which were an ideal background for the dark red three-piece suite and lusciously opulent velvet curtains of olive-green. The carpet was fitted and patterned in a variety of colours, while the remainder of the furniture was a light oak in colour. There was a small foldaway table and chairs, and a small cocktail cabinet. The essence of the room spelled elegant simplicity in design, and it suited Karen's character. She loathed fussy rooms, overflowing with knick-knacks and ornaments of all kinds.

The rest of the flat was composed of her bedroom, a bathroom, a minute kitchen opening off the lounge, and the small studio where she worked, which also opened off the lounge. The studio had roof windows as well as wide windows in the walls and was ideal for working. Here she had her drawing-board, as most of her work was done in the silence of her home.

After her break with Paul she had been left with a lot of spare time in the evenings and had started painting pictures for her own pleasure. It was an entirely new hobby for her and she found great satisfaction in putting her thoughts into paintings. They were, as her mother so unkindly termed them, "ghastly abstracts", and even Lewis showed little interest in them. To him they were so much wasted effort, and he bluntly told her so. Karen was a little disappointed that he should think so, for although she did not believe they were masterpieces, she nevertheless felt that they had something.

All Lewis would admit was that they made her an ideal occupation, but he advised her not to consider them a monetary proposition. As Lewis was a clever designer and knew a lot about art in general, Karen contented herself with his opinion for she did not care much either way. It was merely a means of filling in time.

Now, as she looked round the lounge, the paintings were all about her. As she liked them she had had them framed, and at least they provided a splash of colour on the otherwise bare walls.

She slipped off her overcoat and hung it over a chair, and strolling across the room she took a cigarette from her case and lit it. She thought momentarily that she was smoking far too much, but she drew on the tobacco with enjoyment.

The scarlet telephone on the low table by the couch seemed to mock her silently and she inwardly hated herself for agreeing to her mother's blackmail, as indeed it had been. Telephone Paul or be ostracized.

But how on earth could she just pick up the telephone and speak to a man who had divorced her two years ago and whom she had not spoken to for almost four years? It was ludicrous, really. And would he be secretly amused at her for calling him? What satisfaction would it give him to have her crawling to him for help? She bit her lip angrily. Only her mother could have placed her in such a position. She was tempted to ring Lewis and ask his advice, but decided against it. He would consider her actions quite ridiculous and would most likely advise her not to go through with it.

With a deep sigh she lifted the receiver with trembling fingers and dialled the number of the Frazer building. She knew the number so well; how often had she called Paul there in the old days?

A switchboard operator answered her a few moments later, her cool voice polite and businesslike:

"Frazer Textiles, can I help you?"

"Oh, good morning," said Karen, trying to sound aloof and composed. "Could I speak to Mr. Paul Frazer, please?"

"I'm afraid that's out of the question," replied the operator in her cultured tones. "Mr. Frazer is not in the building, for one thing. Will his personal secretary be able to assist you?"

Karen sighed in annoyance. Her hopes of getting the affair over swiftly were not going to be realized.

"No," she replied, "it's a personal matter, I'm afraid. I don't suppose you could tell me where I can contact Mr. Frazer?"

"Mr. Frazer is touring the factories in Nottingham and Leeds," replied the operator, "but I'm afraid I couldn't tell you where he might be contacted. However, he's expected back in London this evening, I believe he has a board meeting here in the morning."

"Oh!" Karen frowned. Then she would have to wait until the following day. "Thank you. I'll ring again tomorrow."

"Very well, madam." The operator rang off, and Karen replaced her receiver reluctantly. Now that she could not get in touch with him she felt curiously disappointed.

She stared into space for a moment and then on the offchance she dialled his apartment in Belgravia. She knew he lived there now, presumably he had sold the large house, Trevayne, when the divorce came through.

He would want no memories of Karen to mar his future.

She held her breath when someone answered the telephone, but it turned out to be a manservant. He merely repeated what the switchboard operator had told her. Mr. Frazer was in the north of England but would be back this evening. He asked if he could take a message, but Karen said, "No, thank you," and rang off abruptly.

She felt unreasonably angry that he could not be reached. It was absurd to feel that way, she told herself firmly. After all, he might have been out of the country. He often went to Canada and the United States. He could have been there, and then she would have had to have waited for much longer than twenty-four hours. She contemplated calling him that evening, and then vetoed the idea. To call in business hours, calling him at the office, kept things on a strictly business footing. If she rang him that evening it seemed much more personal, and she wanted to maintain the impersonal note in this.

She made herself some scrambled eggs and coffee for lunch and then rang her mother and explained the situation. Madeline Stacey was quite apologetic, but obviously pleased that Karen was doing as she had been asked so precisely and punctually.

Then Karen washed up her few dishes and left them to drain on the draining-board. She had a daily woman, Mrs. Coates, who came in and did her housework for her, but she looked after herself otherwise, making her own meals and taking her washing to the nearby launderette. Her salary was quite adequate to cover these luxuries and Lewis had often suggested that she employ a full-time housekeeper. But Karen preferred her freedom, and as her knowledge of housekeepers was limited to Liza, who ran her mother's life as well as her home, she felt sure she was doing the right thing.

That afternoon, Karen sat staring at her drawing-board finding herself singularly devoid of any ideas. Even her casual paintings held no charm. Outside the apartment a watery sun was shining and it had turned into quite a springlike day. On sudden impulse she left her studio, pulled on her sheepskin coat and left the apartment.

Outside, the air was fresh and invigorating, and she crossed the road into the small park nearby and watched the children playing. It was a favourite spot for nannies with prams and tiny toddlers just learning to run and play with their slightly older brothers and sisters. The sight of the happy, laughing faces turned the knife in Karen's stomach. If she had had the baby Paul had wanted, it would have been three or four years old now. Who knows, she thought dully, she might have had two or even three by this time.

She walked aimlessly across the stretch of grass, wishing the day would end and tomorrow arrive that much sooner. Until she had actually spoken to Paul her concentration was quite non-existent, and if she tried to work in such a manner, it would be a complete waste of time and energy and materials.

She stayed out for a couple of hours and then returned to the flat. She made herself a scratch meal of beans on toast in lieu of dinner, and then switched on the television. It was rarely used, but this evening she enjoyed losing herself in the exciting western and variety show which she watched.

When the television closed down for the night, Karen smoked a last cigarette before going to bed. She thought about Sandra and Simon. Sandra was just foolish enough to get herself into serious trouble. She was completely irresponsible and quite wild, due to her mother's fawnlike adoration all these years. No matter what scrapes she had got into as a child, her mother had always helped her out of them, glossing over the facts to Karen, and consequently now Sandra did not know the meaning of the word sensibility. During Karen's years as Paul's wife, she had been more manageable, owing to Paul's control over her, but after their divorce she had become worse than before.

As for Simon, he ought to have more sense. He and Julia had been rare visitors at Trevayne when Karen was married to Paul. Simon had made it plain from the outset that he favoured his brother's young wife, and Paul had made it equally plain that if Simon came near Karen he would get his head in his hands.

Julia, Simon's wife, had been the daughter of an impoverished earl when she met Simon, and had aroused herself from her rather languid manner long enough to get Simon to marry her. Their parents had approved and Julia, although well aware of Simon's discrepancies, saw in him a meal ticket for life. She enjoyed the company of men, and after their marriage they each went their separate ways to a great extent. They lived in the same house, entertained jointly, but each had their own friends. It was a nauseating set-up, and Paul had avoided them quite openly.

Thinking now of Sandra, throwing herself away on a man like Simon Frazer, disgusted and appalled Karen, and she knew she would be glad if Paul would do something. Only he had the power to dictate to Simon. Paul held the family finances.

Of course, Simon probably gloated over the liaison secretly. He was getting back at Karen and Paul to some measure for having slighted him before. He was an amusing character for all his faults, and no doubt Sandra found him quite fascinating after the rather callow youths she usually associated with.

It was midnight by the time Karen crawled into bed, but sleep did not come easily. Her thoughts were too full of Paul, her mind too active to relax. She recalled how attractive he was, dark-skinned, and dark-haired and dark-eyed. Although she herself was a tall girl, all of five feet seven inches, he absolutely dwarfed her, making her intensely conscious of his overwhelming masculinity. His hair was short and cut close to his head and was always crisp and vital to the touch. His dark eyes, sometimes cynical or amused, could soften miraculously with love, and his mouth had done crazy things to her body. A man of the world before their marriage, he had known many women, but Karen satisfied him mentally as well as physically, and under his tuition she had learned all the delights and desires of her own body.

Remembering all these things disturbed her emotionally, and she moved restlessly in the bed, rolling on to her stomach to stop its churning.

She remembered the nights of the long hot summer that had followed their marriage, when, too hot to sleep, they had gone down to the pool and swum in the moonlight. They had been utterly alone, the rest of the household asleep, and they had made love, their bodies dripping with the cool delicious water.

Groaning, Karen slid wearily out of bed and padded into the bathroom. Filling a tumbler full of water, she extracted a sleeping tablet from the bottle in the cabinet and swallowed it with some of the water. She peered at her weary face in the mirror of the cabinet and frowned. Was she to look like a hag when he saw her tomorrow? Would he be glad he was no longer married to such a tired-looking creature?

She returned slowly to her bed and slid back between the sheets. Moodily, she mused that at least during her marriage to Paul she had never had to resort to sleeping tablets, at least not while they were living together. On the contrary, she had slept soundly and dreamlessly as a child in his arms, conscious of the security of those arms always.

Achingly she stared into space until the cotton wool world of the drug descended upon her and she slept.

She awoke with an aching head next morning, hearing the steady buzz of the vacuum cleaner from the lounge. She slid out of bed and pulled on a blue quilted housecoat before opening the door leading to the lounge.

Mrs. Coates, the daily, was just finishing and she smiled cheerfully at Karen. She was a small, plump woman of about fifty, with a husband and six children at home. She often regaled Karen with stories of "our Bert" or "our Billy", and Karen found her a refreshing personality.

"I've made your coffee," she said now, looking critically at Karen. She nodded towards the kitchen. "You look as though you could do with some."

"Thank you," replied Karen dryly, but padded willingly into the kitchen.

The percolater was bubbling merrily and she poured herself a cup of black coffee and went back into the lounge for her cigarettes.

"Are you all right, dearie?" asked Mrs. Coates, looking worriedly at her.

"Of course. Thank you, Mrs. Coates. I slept rather badly, that's all. I'll be all right when I've had this." She nodded to the coffee.

"Right." Mrs. Coates pulled on her mackintosh. "I'll be off, then. See you in the morning."

"Yes, all right, Mrs. Coates," said Karen, managing a smile, and the woman left.

After she had closed the door, Karen stood down her coffee and walking over to the switch she turned down the temperature of the central heating. Mrs. Coates always kept the place like a greenhouse, and this morning Karen felt as though she needed air, and lots of it.

Her watch told her it was only nine-thirty, so she collected the daily papers, which Mrs. Coates always brought for her, from the kitchen and settled herself on the couch in the lounge.

She knew that Paul would not reach the office until ten o'clock at the earliest, so she read for an hour before tackling the telephone. The newspapers were full of the world crises, but for all the impression they made on her she might just as well not have bothered reading them. Her mind buzzed with the telephone call ahead of her and eventually she laid them aside and merely waited.

Today when the switchboard operator at the Frazer building answered her, Karen again asked for Mr. Frazer and was immediately put through to Paul's office suite.

His private secretary answered her and asked in her cool, modulated voice who was calling and what it was about.

"Mr. Frazer is extremely busy this morning," she continued silkily. "He has a board meeting in half an hour so I'm afraid I must ask you to either call back tomorrow or tell me what it's about. I'm sure I will be able to assist you, whatever it is."

Karen clenched her fingers round the red receiver.

"Just tell Mr. Frazer that Miss Stacey wants to speak to him," she said coolly. "I'm sure he won't refuse to speak to me."

Whether the girl recognized the name herself, Karen couldn't imagine, but after an impatient wait of about five minutes she heard a man's husky voice saying: "Karen, is that you calling?" and she realized it was Paul.

Her heart thumped so loudly she felt sure he must be able to hear it. His voice was so familiar, even after all this time, although it was as cold as a mountain stream.

For a second her nerve almost failed her, and she thought she was not going to be able to go through with it, and then she managed to murmur:

"Yes, it's me. Hello, Paul. How are you?"

Even to her own ears her voice sounded rather nervous and she wished she could be as confident as he sounded.

"I'm very well, thank you," he replied flatly. "Are you?"

"Oh, yes, I'm fine." Karen stiffened her shoulders determinedly.

"That's good," he said, and waited, obviously expecting her to speak and explain why she had called at all. Karen sought about for words to begin the conversation and with cold emphasis Paul said: "Karen, why did you ring me? I'm sure it wasn't simply to ask about the state of my health."

"No," she agreed, sighing.

"Then why?" he asked curtly. "Come on, Karen. I'm a busy man."

Karen gasped. How dared he speak to her like that? In that superior tone! All of a sudden her courage returned. His manner had caught her on the raw and she was damned if he was going to treat her like dirt.

"I'm afraid I cannot discuss it over the telephone," she replied icily. She had been going to tell him a little of the matter over the phone and suggest that they meet to discuss the rest, but now she decided he could wait and find out what she wanted. "It's a personal matter," she continued, "I should like to see you."

"I can't imagine what we have to say to one another," he replied coolly.

Karen tried to control her rising temper. She felt much better about everything now. He was just as belligerent as ever. No doubt he thought that she wanted to talk to him about Ruth.

"Paul," she said carefully, in a controlled voice, "this matter concerns two other people, not ourselves, so don't think for one moment that I'm trying to make an assignation with you."

Paul sighed. "I don't understand a word of this, Karen. Why can't you tell me now?"

Karen sighed herself. "Good lord, Paul, just take my word that it concerns you just as much as me."

"And when do you suggest we meet?" he asked.

"How about lunch?"

"Today? God, Karen, I only arrived back from Leeds last night. I'm absolutely up to my eyes in work."

"Oh, dear." Karen sounded sarcastic. "But then, even tycoons have to eat sometimes, don't they? Or do you live on vitamin pills these days?"

Paul was silent for a moment and she heard him flicking over the papers on his desk.

"Make up your mind," she said abruptly.

"All right," he said slowly. "I suppose I can make it."

"Don't put yourself out," she exclaimed heatedly.

He sounded almost amused. "Still the same old Karen," he remarked cynically. "Will one o'clock at Stepano's suit you? I have a table there."

"Admirably," she replied dryly, and rang off.

As she lit a cigarette she found she was trembling again. This would never do. She hated herself for becoming so emotionally involved. After all, it was only a luncheon appointment, not a visit to the torture chamber.

She spent a long time deciding what she would wear. She needed something smart but not too dressy. Certainly nothing to make him imagine this was anything other than a business engagement. On the other hand, she wanted to look her best, if only to show him how well she was managing alone.

Black was the best idea, she decided at last, and chose a close-fitting black suit which suited her very fair colouring to perfection. The neckline of the suit was low and round, and she added a string of pearls, which he had bought her for their first wedding anniversary, to complete the ensemble. She never wore a hat and her thick, straight hair needed no adornment. It tip-tilted slightly at the ends and was so soft and silky that it always looked attractive. Paul had always admired her hair, the jagged fringe straying across her wide brow and framing her piquantly attractive face.

She studied her face in the mirror for a moment when she was ready, wondering whether she had changed. Her best features were her eyes, framed by thick black lashes that needed no mascara. Her eyes were greeny-grey and very widely spaced, while her nose was small and slightly retroussé. Her mouth was full and passionate and much too big in her estimation. However, she sighed, she was as she was and nothing could change that.

She took a taxi to Stepano's. The traffic in London at lunchtime was such that to take her own car would have been a futile effort. Besides she hated driving in the rat-race of vehicles, always conscious of the swarm of cars on her tail, ready to pounce if she made a mistake.

Stepano's was a massive, glass-fronted restaurant in Oxford Street. Karen had never been inside before, but as she entered she was greeted by a white-coated waiter who escorted her with reverence to Paul's table. Paul had not yet arrived and Karen ordered a dry Martini and lit a cigarette.

As she sipped her drink her eyes surveyed the large dining-room with its gleaming damask cloths, shining silver and hot-house flowers. The clientele matched their surroundings, over-indulged, expense-account fed men and elegantly jewelled women. There were some younger people, but even they were all too obviously bored by too much of everything. However, she was aware that she too was being studied and discussed. After all, this was Paul Frazer's table and she was not the woman with whom he had been photographed so frequently lately. She wondered if any of them recognized her as Paul's ex-wife. She felt quite amused as she imagined their comments if they did.

At five past one, the swing glass doors opened to admit, Paul Frazer. He was dressed in a camel-hair overcoat, which he removed and gave to the waiter who hovered at his side. Underneath he was wearing a charcoal grey lounge suit of impeccable cut, and he looked bigger and broader than she remembered. Even so, he did not look to have an ounce of spare flesh on him. He was big-framed and muscular, and as she watched him thread his way through the tables to his own, she was intensely conscious of the almost animal magnetism about him which had so thrilled her in the old days. He walked with a lithe, easy grace for such a big man, passing a word here and there with acquaintances he knew. His hair was still as thick and black as ever, only lightly touched with grey at the temples, which served to give him a distinguished appearance. He was still as lazily attractive as ever and at thirty-seven looked the well-dressed, assured business tycoon that he was. If he had grown a little more cynical with the years that was only to be expected of a man with his wealth and position, who knew that money could buy most things he wanted.

He reached the table and seated himself opposite her with a brief nod. Conscious that they were the cynosure of all eyes, Karen flushed and looked down at her drink.

"Well, Karen," he murmured lightly, "you haven't changed much. Still as beautiful as ever, and as talented too, I hear."

Karen looked up at him and for a moment his dark eyes held hers. Then with a rush she said:

"Thank you, Paul. You haven't changed, either. Are you still working hard, too?"

He half smiled in a mocking manner. "I was, until I was dragged to a certain luncheon appointment."

Karen looked indignantly at him. "You need not have come," she stated abruptly, colouring.

"Oh, really? With you flinging innuendoes left, right and centre? Besides, you set out to make me curious and you succeeded. That should please you."

The wine waiter appeared by his side and he ordered himself a whisky and another Martini for Karen. After the wine waiter had left, the head waiter arrived for their order, and Paul took the menu and ordered for them both as he had always done in the past.

When his whisky had been supplied together with Karen's Martini and they were waiting for the first course to be served, he said:

"No retaliation yet. I felt sure you were thinking up some vitriolic reply while I studied the food."

"Don't be so clever," she retorted, disliking his mocking treatment of her. "I ought to be congratulating you on your engagement, but I won't."

"Thank you, all the same. Was that what you wanted to talk about?"

Karen gasped. "I told you it had nothing to do with us," she snapped angrily.

Paul shrugged, and iced melon was served. Karen felt

singularly unhungry, which was quite unusual for her, and only toyed with the food.

Paul ate his and then said: "Well, come on, then. Don't keep me in suspense."

Karen pushed her plate away.

"My ... my mother asked me to speak to you," she began slowly.

"Oh. I see. And how is Madeline these days?" He swallowed the remainder of his drink. "I keep meaning to visit her."

"She's all right," replied Karen, glad of the brief diversion. "I'm sure she'd be overjoyed to see you. You were always her blue-eyed boy, in a manner of speaking, of course." This last because she knew his eyes were a very dark grey so as to appear almost black at times.

"Good." He raised his eyebrows. "Well ... go on."

Karen reluctantly continued. "It's really about Sandra that I wanted to speak to you," she said.

"Why? Does she need money or something?"

"No," retorted Karen shortly. "Money; the be-all and end-all of everything to you, I suppose."

"It helps," he remarked sardonically.

"Anyway, it's not money. Sandra is going around with Simon ... your dear brother Simon, that is."

"Simon?" echoed Paul, all mockery gone from his voice. "Good lord, is she completely out of her mind? Simon's years older than her, and he's married into the bargain."

Karen sighed and nodded. "I know that and you know that, but Sandra apparently, doesn't. You know how wilful she is, how wild and uncontrollable. Goodness knows what trouble she'll get herself into. She's stupid enough to allow him enough licence to ... well, you know Sandra ... and Simon."

Paul nodded and looked thoughtfully down at the salmon which had been placed before him.

"She needs a damn good hiding," he muttered violently.

"Precisely, but no one is likely to give it to her," said Karen moodily.

Paul shrugged. "So. What am I expected to do about it?"

"You know what Simon is like," said Karen, looking at him earnestly. "And you can handle him. You've told me so numerous times. We want you to stop him seeing her. She won't take any notice of us, and short of locking her up every night, there's very little we can do."

"I see. So you want me to play the heavy father! How?"

Karen flushed. "You employ him. You dictate his income. He has no money of his own to speak of. I know that."

"Hmn. You've got it all worked out, haven't you?" he remarked dryly.

Karen clenched her fingers round her knife and fork. His voice was mocking again and she hated the humble position she had put herself into.

"And ... er ... why should I do this?" he asked annoyingly. "I mean, Simon is free, white, and over twenty-one. If Sandra is reckless enough to go out with him, oughtn't she to bear the consequences?"

"Yes, she ought," exclaimed Karen hotly. "And if I had my way, I would never have asked you to do anything. My mother bribed me into doing this by one of her devious methods and at the moment I couldn't care less what you do."

He smiled. "Do keep your voice down, Karen, or do you want the whole restaurant to hear our discussion? It would make a charming topic of conversation at cocktails this evening."

"Oh, you're hateful!" she cried, feeling as though she might burst into tears at any moment.

"Relax," he remarked abruptly. "Your mission is accomplished. I'll speak to brother Simon. If only to keep you in good stead with your mother."

"Thank you," she muttered, and thereafter ate in

silence. She was conscious of his speculative gaze on her often during the course of the meal and to her ignominy, her face refused to resume its normal colour and remained flushed.

When the meal was over and coffee was served. Paul offered Karen a cigarette and after he had lit hers and his own he said:

"You're still with Lewis Martin, then." It was more of a statement than a question.

'Yes. Lewis and I get on very well," she replied coldly.

' I'm sure you do," he agreed smoothly. "Why haven't you married him?"

"Because I haven't," she retorted. "In any case, it's no concern of yours."

"Of course not. I was merely making conversation." He smiled mockingly and she conveyed her own gaze to the tip of her cigarette.

"How . . . how is your mother?" she asked quietly.

Paul's mother lived in the South of France. When her husband died and Paul took over the business, she had retired there to live with her sister and Paul and Karen had visited her a couple of times during their marriage. Karen had liked her but had not had a lot to do with her.

"She's very well," answered Paul gravely. "I expect Ruth and I will stay there for a while after the wedding."

"Does Ruth already know your mother?"

"She has met her, yes. She flew over for the engagement party."

"Ah, yes. I ought to have remembered," said Karen, shrugging. "And when is the wedding to be?" The question was a tortuous one for her. Asking when Paul intended to make another woman his wife.

"In about three months," he replied smoothly. "Ruth wants to be a June bride."

"How sweet," remarked Karen sardonically. "I'm

sure she'll do you credit."

"I'm sure she will," he said easily. "She's a very attractive person."

Karen drew on her cigarette. She had only seen a photograph of Ruth in a newspaper and really it had not given much life to her features.

"Do you intend living at the apartment, afterwards?" she asked, wanting to know and yet dreading the answer.

"To begin with, perhaps," he replied, dropping a sliver of ash into the silver ashtray. "I expect I shall buy a house, somewhere in the country. Ruth knows England quite well and likes the Weald."

"Oh yes? How nice for you both." Karen sounded bored by it all.

Paul shrugged. "I'm sure it will be. And then of course, we will spend some time each year in America. Ruth's family live in Dallas."

Karen finished her coffee. "And you're having a honeymoon, too, I suppose?"

Paul smiled. "You're very curious about us, aren't you?"

"Why not?" She managed a tight smile. "What else is there to talk about?"

"We may go touring," he remarked slowly. "We haven't decided yet. Ruth adores being the perfect tourist."

"Touring?" exclaimed Karen, raising her dark eyebrows. "That's rather a strenuous way to spend your honeymoon." She smiled suddenly, remembering. "Do you recall the months we spent in that villa near Nassau, with that gorgeous beach all to ourselves?"

Paul frowned and stubbed out his cigarette. "Yes, I remember," he replied, his voice cold. Karen looked surprised and yet felt reasonably pleased. He had been so complacent, so confident, but the mention of their honeymoon still had the power to disturb him. Those halcyon days and nights were never to be forgotten, whatever

Ruth might have to offer, and even Paul had to acknowledge this to himself.

Studying him when he was not aware of her doing so, she found repugnance in the very idea of his marrying another woman. After all, their marriage had seemed so right at first and seeing him now brought it home to her that divorce inevitably changes everything completely. She felt she wanted to reach across to him and have him look at her as he had used to look at her with love in his eyes. She wanted to tell him she still loved him and would go back to him today if he would have her.

But that awful thing called civilized conduct prevented her from doing such a thing and instead they exchanged platitudes and ignored the primitive emotions working beneath the surface.

They finished their coffee and Paul said:

"I'm afraid I must go now. I have a great deal to do this afternoon and I have a business engagement at three."

Karen rose to her feet. "That's quite all right, Paul. I've said what I came to say."

Paul shrugged almost imperceptibly and then stood back to allow her to precede him from the room. Once outside, he pulled on his overcoat and said:

"My car is parked nearby. Can I drop you anywhere?"

Karen hesitated for a moment. She had no desire to prolong the agony, but she did intend going to see Lewis this afternoon, and now was as good a time as any.

"You could take me to Martin's," she said, looking up at him with a cool green gaze. "I want to see Lewis." She said the latter part purposely and was amused when his face darkened slightly. It lasted only a moment and then it was gone, and he was nodding and assisting her down the shallow steps to the pavement.

The car was not far away and they walked towards it in silence. Karen had never seen this car before. It was a low-slung, continental car in cream with scarlet upholstery, and when Karen was put inside she found it superbly comfortable. The springing of the seats was luxuriously soft and it was like gliding on a bed of feathers.

"A new car," she murmured softly. "Very elegant."

Paul shrugged and slid behind the wheel, his thigh brushing hers for a moment, causing Karen to shiver slightly.

"I'm glad you like it. It suits me. It's good for acceleration purposes which is what I need for some of the roads I have to cover."

"It makes my old rattletrap seem very old and outmoded. But I like the old bus and it serves its purpose. I don't use it such a lot." Karen grimaced.

Paul glanced swiftly at her. "But you could afford a new one, couldn't you?" It was a statement rather than a question.

Karen half smiled. "Of course," she admitted easily. "But I don't want one just at the moment. Oh, don't worry, honey, I'm not a pauper yet, not by any means. Sorry to disappoint you."

Paul flushed. "Why say something like that?" he muttered, "I don't want to see you without means. Good heavens, I would be quite willing to help you if ever you needed money, surely you know that?"

Karen's eyes widened. "Do I? Why should you imagine I would come to you for anything?"

Paul looked amused. "Well, haven't you done just that thing?"

Karen flushed. "Very clever," she said, annoyed with herself for being so rash. "Come on, let's go."

Paul shrugged and drove out into the stream of traffic.

Martin Textile Designs stood in a by-road off Great Portland Street. It was a tall, imposing building, although the basement and first floor were merely warehouses for another company. Lewis Martin's domain occupied the upper floors with Lewis's office being at the top. Karen had a small office of her own there, but she seldom used it, preferring to work at home.

Paul drew the large automobile to a halt at the entrance and said:

"I guess this is it," in a lazy voice.

"Yes. Thank you for the lift," said Karen politely, and made to get out.

"I'll ring you as soon as I have any information," said Paul, nodding.

Karen inclined her head and slid out on to the pavement.

"Thank you for lunch," she said, rather sardonically. "I'm sorry I had to drag you away from your business."

"It was a pleasure," replied Paul, just as mockingly. "Be good," and he put the car into gear and moved swiftly away before Karen could make some cutting retort.

Fuming, Karen walked into the building and entering the lift pressed the button for the fourth floor. As the lift went on its way she lit a cigarette and drew deeply on it. He was so assured, so confident and oh! so detached. She felt quite angry and she longed to be able to do something to shatter his complacency. How calmly he had discussed Ruth and his forthcoming marriage. How amused he had been at her obvious curiosity. Would he tell Ruth about it? Maybe laugh with her about Karen's forced need of his help? She felt as though something shrivelled up inside her. To think of them together, discussing her, was disgusting and depressing. How aloof he seemed from the rigours of a disastrous love affair. How composed about his life with Ruth. With Karen he had had sometimes to bend his will to hers. With Ruth he would hold the upper hand and being the feminine creature she apparently was, she would enjoy letting him be the master. They would have no fierce arguments or even differences of opinion. She would be completely attuned to his every desire and act likewise. But surely, thought Karen desperately, that would become boring in time to a man like Paul. Variety was the spice of life and he needed someone to oppose him at times. At least so she had thought. Of course, if he got bored, he could always find himself another woman, and probably Ruth would not object too strongly if he kept it quiet. Karen stamped on the butt of her cigarette and ground it into the flooring with her heel. The lift reached the fourth floor. She had arrived.

She entered the outer office of Lewis's domain and asked his secretary if he was free.

"Yes, Miss Stacey," she replied, smiling. "Go right in. He is expecting you."

Karen lightly tapped on Lewis's door and then entered his office. It was not a large office but the wide windows gave the room plenty of light, giving an impression of space. Lewis himself was seated at his desk, studying some papers, and he looked up as she entered, a smile spreading over his face. He was a man of medium height, slimly built, with greying blond hair. He spent his leisure hours reading and writing articles for trade papers and consequently his eyes behind their horn-rimmed spectacles looked rather tired. But he was obviously pleased to see her, and she closed the door and advanced into the room, sinking down into a low armchair opposite him.

Perceptively, he said: "You look rather disturbed. What's been going on?"

Karen flung herself back in the chair, helping herself to another cigarette. As she lit the cigarette and looked at Lewis, she thought reflectively that the contrast between Paul and Lewis was very considerable. Not only in looks but in manner.

"Let me relax for a moment and then I'll tell you," she said, managing a rather grim smile.

After drawing on her cigarette for about five minutes, during which time Lewis studied his papers and considerately ignored her, she said:

"I've just had lunch with my esteemed ex-husband."

A strange expression flitted across Lewis's face for a moment and then he said:

"You must be joking."

"No, I'm not," she replied smoothly. "Dear Paul himself."

Lewis compressed his rather thin lips.

"And what was this in aid of?" He shrugged his slim shoulders.

"I . . . I asked him to see me, have lunch with me," answered Karen, half amused at Lewis's concern. He could see no reason, until she told him, for the meeting and he was getting quite annoyed.

His eyebrows ascended. "You asked him to meet you. But why? Good lord, Karen, you aren't trying to get him back, are you?"

Karen looked away from his gaze. She wondered what he would think if he could have read her thoughts a few moments ago. He would be bound to be furious. After all, he had thought he was acting in her best interests when he helped her to avoid seeing Paul.

Avoiding this question, she said: "Mother asked me to see him. Simon, his brother Simon that is, is going out with Sandra, and Sandra refuses to give him up. I had to appeal to Paul to prevent it going any further."

"Sandra!" exclaimed Lewis. "But Simon Frazer is married. Is she completely mad? Good heavens, he's nothing but a scoundrel."

"Precisely . . . but you know how unmanageable Sandra is. She's gradually becoming completely uncontrollable. Besides. Mother still dotes on her and indulges her in everything. Even now, I expect she's worried to death in case Sandra finds out she's been meddling."

Lewis rose restlessly to his feet. "But to ask you to see Frazer on her behalf. She ought to have more sense. Doesn't she care who gets hurt in all this? She might have realized that he would take a delight in humiliating you."

Karen stretched her slim legs out in front of her. "Paul didn't exactly humiliate me, darling. In fact, he was quite human about the whole thing. But on the other hand, I can imagine what he was thinking. He probably thought I'd seen his engagement in the paper and decided to make a bit of bother for him. I don't really think he thought I was trying to get him back. I think if anything, he thought I was just being nosy."

"Are you seeing him again?" asked Lewis, frowning.

"I doubt it," replied Karen abruptly. "I expect he will ring me if he has any news about Simon and Sandra."

"Well, I sincerely hope so," said Lewis, sighing with something like relief. "After all, we don't want him causing you any more bother, do we?"

"I should say that's entirely unlikely," remarked Karen wryly. "He seems completely absorbed with Ruth and their forthcoming marriage."

Lewis nodded. "I believe she's quite a lovely girl," he said, and then clasped his hands together. "Oh, my dear, I hope you don't think I'm trying to upset you."

"Not at all," replied Karen, rather dryly, wishing Lewis had not found it necessary to discuss Ruth at all.

"You know I'd like to take care of you," went on Lewis painfully. "I want to be able to have the right to do that. "Won't you allow me ...'

"Lewis, please. Not now. I've told you so often, I don't love you and I couldn't marry someone I didn't love. The very idea appals me. I like and respect you, but as yet I don't feel I can love anybody." But Paul, taunted her conscience, but she thrust the thought back into anonymity.

Lewis became businesslike, and Karen appreciated it. He was always so understanding. If he had behaved in any other way she would have had to find herself another employer, and as they worked so well together she didn't want to have to do that.

"By the way," he said at the end of their discussion, "I have two invitations for the charity ball at the Magnifique on Friday. Would you like to go? It should be quite a glittering affair. Take you out of yourself."

Karen hesitated. She usually refused these invitations

point-blank, but today, after Lewis's understanding manner, she felt she ought to give them both a break. After all, maybe he was right. A ball would take her out of herself and perhaps push her feelings for Paul back into perspective.

"Well," she began slowly, "I think perhaps it might be a good idea, Lewis. Thank you."

Lewis looked absolutely flabbergasted, and she smiled at his shocked face.

"Didn't you really want me to come?" she asked, teasing him.

"Good lord, yes. It's just that I didn't hold out much hope and now that you've accepted I'm stunned!"

Karen smiled. "Oh, well I feel I should come out of my shell for a change. I've been too reticent of late." She shivered involuntarily. In a matter of hours her life seemed to have changed. She had been content to drift along in her own backwater, letting life pass her by. Suddenly she had found her own company uncongenial and the thought of dressing up and going out, no matter with whom, gave her something to think about.

"A good idea," approved Lewis, smiling. "I'm glad you feel you want to meet people again. That's a good sign."

Karen nodded. "Yes, isn't it? Perhaps seeing Paul has done me good. After all, that's over and done with now, isn't it?" she said, forcing a lightness she did not feel.

Lewis looked very pleased. Suddenly his rather dull day had improved beyond all expectation.

CHAPTER TWO

AFTER Paul Frazer had dropped Karen at the offices of Lewis Martin's company he drove swiftly back to his own office building. In truth there was a lot of work waiting for him, but now his urge to get on and get it done had turned sour on him. He couldn't understand it. It was maddening. His thoughts were in a turmoil. Seeing Karen had been something he had never expected to have to go through. Although she had killed the love he had felt for her, she still had the power to disturb him emotionally, and it infuriated him. After all, he had met many more beautiful women in his lifetime, what was it about Karen that so enthralled him?

In truth he had forgotten just how attractive she really was, and to be confronted with her so unexpectedly had had no little effect on him. He went up to his office in a rare bad humour and was surprised when he found Ruth waiting in his office for him. Ruth had never come to the office before, and now that she had he felt annoyed for some reason. He refused to connect this feeling with his earlier meeting with his ex-wife.

Ruth was a small curvaceous brunette with short hair cropped in a curly mop. She always looked bandbox-fresh and favoured very feminine styles, with flared skirts that accentuated her petiteness. She was twenty-eight, but appeared younger, and until today Paul had found this refreshing.

But after Karen's deliberate reference to their honeymoon in Nassau, all the details of their previous relationship had been recollected with piercing clarity. She had recalled memories which he had believed were completely forgotten, and yet one word from her had revived everything. She had made him aware of her as a woman, a tantalizing woman. She had always had a devastating effect on him from the very first moment she had entered his office with the design manager to be complimented on her original carpet design.

At first, her apparent beauty and charm had appealed to him, but as he got to know her better he had fallen in love with her for the intelligent woman that she was; young, vital, desirable and able to converse with him on any subject he cared to bring up. He had always had his pick of attractive women. He was well aware that his money added to his own eligibility, and when Karen refused to enter into an affair with him he found it quite a novel experience. Usually, girls had been all too willing to sleep with him, and it piqued him to find that Karen could refuse. It annoyed him, too, to find that his interest in other women had waned and he knew that only Karen could satisfy him now. As the weeks passed he came to need her more than anyone else in the world and he knew she reciprocated his feelings but only marriage would satisfy her. But strangely, he found he did not mind, and those first few months of their marriage fulfilled all his wildest dreams.

But when she defied him and went behind his back to get a job with Lewis Martin he had been infuriated, and later when the final break came he was sick to his stomach. He would never have believed she could hurt him so and when Martin averred that she did not wish to see him ever again, he had given up hope.

At first he had lost a lot of weight, for he had eaten little and drank a lot. He suffered from acute insomnia for months, and life had lost all interest. In consequence his work suffered and eventually his mother had persuaded him to take a prolonged holiday, for as he was he was of no use to the company.

When he had first been informed of her affair with Lewis Martin, he had hardly believed it. He could not acknowledge to himself that Karen would actually sleep with another man, particularly a man like Martin who was so much older than herself. Thoughts of them together had nauseated him and angered him. He was still so much in love with Karen, and if she had shown any inclinations towards coming back to him he would have accepted her on any terms.

But when he learned that Lewis Martin had actually spent a night at the apartment, he was forced to admit that all previous stories about them had been true, and their marriage was over, irrevocably. He drank a good deal at this time, drugging his tortured senses, until the pull of his work brought him back to normality.

The divorce, of course, finalized everything. It was the ultimate ending. The writing on the wall had eventually triumphed. Paul had been convinced that no woman would ever invade his emotions again. He became very cynical about life and women, and lived without much thought for the morrow.

And then, six months ago, he had met Ruth Delaney. They met at a cocktail party in New York where he was attending a textile trade fair. She had immediately made a beeline for him, realizing he was the most attractive male she had ever seen or was ever likely to see. His cynical manner had added a rather cruel twist to his lips and he was leaner than he had been before the divorce, and very bitter. She became his shadow, appearing at all the functions he attended, until he was forced to take notice of her. After all, her father was Hiram Delaney, an oil magnate, and his money might help the company if nothing else, Paul's public relations officer had urged him to be sociable to the Americans, and Paul found it comparatively easy to comply. Ruth was a likeable girl, and her youthful aura was what he needed to brighten his image.

To begin with, Paul had merely used her, taking advantage of her naiveté, but gradually she worked her way into his confidence, and eventually he told her about his broken marriage. Ruth was very sympathetic. She commiserated with him and made him aware of himself as a comparatively young man without much point to his life. Paul was quite aware that Ruth intended that she herself should become the point in his life.

She was devoted to him, and when he returned to London she prevailed upon her parents to visit there too. Consequently, Paul found himself with three guests, at least two of whom expected him to marry Ruth. He was being politely managed, and he allowed himself to drift with the tide. When the tide became a tidal wave and an engagement was quite essential to keep harmony, he decided that as he would never love again he might as well provide himself with a wife and hostess and later, if children came along, the tragedy of his earlier marriage might disappear. So he and Ruth became engaged and her parents, satisfied at last, returned to the States leaving Ruth in Paul's care.

Today Ruth was wearing a mink coat and a very feminine hat of pink feathers. She looked chic and very expensive, but Paul sighed deeply as she rose to meet him. She had been sitting in the chair used by clients, at the far side of his desk, and she moved towards him in a cloud of exotic French perfume.

"Hello, darling," she said reproachfully. "You didn't tell me you were to be out for lunch. I've been waiting here for almost an hour."

Paul allowed her lips to touch his cheek before moving away, removing his overcoat.

"Really," he said. "I'm sorry, Ruth. I had no alternative, I'm afraid."

He dropped his coat on to a low couch and then crossing to his desk, he flung himself into the chair behind it, reaching for his cigarette case.

Ruth lifted his overcoat with a knowing smile, and hung it on the stand before resuming her seat opposite him.

"Now," she murmured, "what on earth was so important that you had to drop everything and go out to lunch? When I asked you yesterday evening you said you would have no time for anything."

"That was quite true," replied Paul, drawing on his cigarette. Ruth did not smoke.

"Well, come on," said Ruth. "Why are you looking so moody and disgruntled? You seem hardly pleased to see me."

Paul shrugged. "I'm sorry, Ruth," he murmured, frowning. "I was just thinking."

Ruth pulled a face and stared at him through her deep brown eyes.

"I had lunch with Karen," he said at length.

"Karen?" Ruth's eyes became saucers. "Not ... not ...?"

"My ex-wife? Yes, I'm afraid so."

Ruth was absolutely astounded and looked it. Until now, Karen had always seemed a phantom figure, vaguely there in the background but unsubstantial.

"And what she had to say to you was highly important, I suppose?" Ruth exclaimed, gathering her startled wits. She clenched her fists. What did this mean? Surely he wasn't intending to get involved with Karen again? For the first time she began to wonder just what Karen was really like. Paul had never described her and she had never been really interested.

"Yes, it was," he said slowly. "Her sister Sandra, who is seventeen, is running around with Simon ... brother Simon, that is."

Ruth's tense nerves relaxed a little.

"But, Paul, Simon is a married man! Why, I met Julia for lunch only last week. She didn't lead me to believe that they were splitting up."

Paul's cynical expression hardened. "My dear Ruth," he exclaimed, shaking his head, "they have no intention of splitting up. Simon does this all the time. So does Julia, for that matter. They have a very comfortable arrangement, I believe."

Ruth flushed, and compressed her rather thin lips.

"You must be joking!"

"Must I?" He smiled wryly. "Life has obviously

shielded you from any unpleasantness, Ruth. Grow up! These affairs happen all the time."

"Well, I think it's disgusting," she cried, biting her lip. "This is the twentieth century! People don't have lovers and mistresses any more. Two people, like ourselves, may meet and discover in time whether we're suitably matched, but acting like this – well – it's animalistic ... barely civilized!"

Paul shrugged. "I know what a womanizer Simon must seem to you, but his private life is usually no concern of mine. As long as his work doesn't suffer in consequence, he can do as he likes as far as I'm concerned. However, in this instance it's rather different. Karen has asked me to intercede on her mother's behalf. Sandra is young and foolish. Wild, if you like. But she's taking on more than she can cope with, if she takes on Simon."

Ruth snorted angrily. She objected to Karen's almost proprietorial use of her ex-husband.

"If this Sandra is anything like Karen, then I should imagine she's well able to take care of herself," she remarked angrily. "She probably deserves anything she gets."

Paul's face grew cold and Ruth knew she had said the wrong thing.

"And just what do you know about Karen?" he asked coldly.

Ruth stretched her fingers and allowed her eyes to gloat on the emerald engagement ring sparkling on her finger.

"Julia has told me quite a lot about Karen," she replied, half defensively.

Paul stubbed out his cigarette.

"Indeed? I never knew you had such cosy chats together. You must tell me more."

Ruth flushed. "Paul, don't be mad. Julia hasn't told anything more than I suspected from your own words on the subject. For goodness' sake, it's over now. I'm sorry if I spoke out of turn, but you're not her slave any longer."

Paul shrugged.

"I suggest, then, that you forget anything Julia has told you about Karen. She knows only too well that Karen is twice the woman she will ever be and also that Simon has always made it clear that Karen intrigued him. Oh, I know he has other women, but Julia never knows who they are. It was quite a blow to find him trying to make headway with his brother's wife. The stigma has remained."

Ruth's flush deepened. "All right, all right, Paul. She must be quite a woman." This last was said rather sarcastically.

"Yes," murmured Paul thoughtfully, and then Ruth returned to the attack.

"Well, anyway, why couldn't she have telephoned you, or even her mother could have phoned?"

"She did telephone, but I did not choose to discuss personal family affairs through the medium of a telephone, the privacy of which is doubtful."

Ruth shrugged.

"I suppose you're right," she replied coolly. "So you had a cosy lunch together?"

Paul smiled dryly. "I should hardly have described it as cosy," he said reflectively.

Ruth rose to her feet. "Well, that's that, then. I suppose you're going to play the heavy father with Simon."

"I shall try. Sandra used to be a nice kid. Spoilt, I admit, but pleasant. I wouldn't like to see anything happen to her."

Ruth bit her lip again. She didn't like this conversation. Her visit to the office had been intended to relieve the monotony of Paul's otherwise dull day. Instead, she had been kept hanging around for an hour and now he had returned all he could talk about was Karen. She felt utterly and reasonably depressed. She liked to think of herself as the only woman in Paul's life. What was past was past, and she was the present. His broken marriage had been the result of foolish impulsiveness and she wanted to be the wife he adored. She had no intention of being bored. Indeed, she was convinced that life with a man like Paul could never be boring.

Paul looked up at her wearily.

"Don't worry," he remarked dryly. "Karen isn't interested in me, Ruth. She's still working for Lewis Martin and I imagine they will be getting married one day. It amazes me that they haven't done so already. I expected it as soon as the divorce became absolute."

Ruth noticed that he did not say he was not interested in her, but decided to refrain from mentioning this. After all, he couldn't be, could he? If he had been surely he would have tried to get her back. No, he loved her, Ruth. He would not let Karen make a fool of him a second time, she was convinced of that. His pride, if nothing else, would prevent it.

"I'm so glad," she remarked, and felt herself relaxing a little. "Now, where are we going tonight? That is, if you can drag yourself away from the office."

Paul's eyes narrowed enigmatically, and she could not tell what he was thinking.

"Where would you like to go?" he asked, running a hand through his thick hair.

Ruth shrugged. "The opera ... play?"

"Good. I'll get Miss Hopper to get tickets. I'll pick you up at your hotel later and we'll have dinner first. Does that suit you?"

"Marvellously," agreed Ruth enthusiastically. Now they were back on ground she knew, not treading among old unexploded mines. "By the way, darling," she continued, "I've got some tickets for the charity ball at the Magnifique on Friday. It sounds exciting. I'm looking forward to it."

Just at the moment Paul felt absolutely no interest in a ball.

He frowned and said, temporizing: "I don't usually attend those functions, Ruth. I buy tickets, of course, but ..."

"But nothing, Paul," she exclaimed. "I'd like to go. Doesn't that mean anything to you?"

Paul felt uncomfortably aware of behaving boorishly.

"Of course it does," he said placatingly. "I'm sorry, Ruth. Of course we'll go if that's what you want."

Ruth smiled triumphantly, assured again of her position.

"Thank you, darling," she said, "and now I'll go and let you go on. I've wasted enough of your time."

After Ruth had gone, Paul buried his head in his hands. His thoughts were chaotic and not pleasant. It was degrading to feel this way and he was furious with himself for feeling so. It had been a strange and unreal day and the strain had been greater than he had thought possible.

With a sigh he lit another cigarette and crossing to a filing cabinet he withdrew a bottle of Scotch and a glass. He poured himself a stiff drink and then reseated himself at his desk. He couldn't help recalling how unalike Ruth and Karen were. It was remarkable, really. Ruth was small whereas Karen was tall and almost voluptuous. Ruth wore her hair short and curly, Karen's was long and straight. Ruth favoured feminine, fussy clothes, whereas Karen preferred casual attire and suited slacks and sweaters. Surely it must mean something. He smiled to himself. No doubt a psychiatrist would tell him it was a form of mental aberration. Probably it was. Probably his subconscious rejected any similarities between the woman he had divorced and the woman he intended to marry. But no matter what happened, Karen was not going to insinuate herself into his life a second time. He had Ruth who loved him selflessly, who would never demand anything from him that he was not prepared to give; who would bear his children with love and never want to be something she was not. If his own feelings were not seriously involved so much the better. Sexual attraction could be hell as well as ecstasy.

Karen was dressing on Thursday morning, two days later, when the telephone suddenly pealed shrilly. It was only ten-fifteen, and Mrs. Coates had just gone. Karen pulled on her housecoat over her underclothes and rushed across to the telephone. She wondered breathlessly whether it would be Paul.

She picked up the phone and gave her number.

"Is that you, Karen?" came a male voice – one she recognized at once was not Paul's.

"Yes," she said, with some curiosity. "Who's that?"

"Don't you remember me? I'm heartbroken," he replied mockingly, and she suddenly knew who it was.

"What on earth do you want, Simon?" she asked resignedly, recognizing the voice of Paul's brother. "Where ever are you at this early hour?"

"I'm in the lobby, downstairs," he replied easily. "I want to see you. Can I come up?"

"I suppose so," she said, sighing. "But I'm not dressed yet, give me a few moments."

"I'll be right up," he answered abruptly, and rang off.

Karen bit her lip and replaced the receiver. What on earth could Simon want with her? He had never contacted her before. Since the divorce she had hardly seen him and never more than accidentally. Did he want to discuss Sandra? She hoped not. She was just hoping that Paul had settled all that himself.

She had barely turned round before there was a knock at her door. Exasperated, she wrapped the housecoat closer about her and went to the door. She looked warmly beautiful, the deep blue of the housecoat accentuating her absolute fairness. Simon was leaning against the doorpost and his eyes lit up appreciatively at the sight of her. She had always intrigued him, but had made it clear from the beginning that she thought little of him. He was five years older than she was but acted about ten years younger at times. He was a thinner, more self-indulged version of Paul, with dark hair that needed cutting at the moment, and a rather sallow complexion through not getting enough fresh air. She supposed he was an attractive man, but she felt sure the weakness in his face and the sensuality of his mouth would have revolted her, had she had anything further to do with him. Many women had fallen victim to his charms, but they were women like himself usually, who lived for the day and had no thought for tomorrow. This affair with Sandra was a new departure for him, and Karen felt infuriated that Sandra couldn't see him for the weak-kneed individual he was.

"Well?" she said uncompromisingly. "What do you want?"

"Oh, come now," he exclaimed reproachfully. "Surely you're going to ask me in? I assure you I haven't come to rape you, whatever you may think."

Karen sighed heavily, and then stepped back to allow him to enter the apartment.

"Very nice," he murmured as he strolled over to the couch and lounged on to it. "You certainly have a nice place here, Karen."

"Cut the preliminaries," said Karen abruptly. "Just state your business and go."

But Simon was not so eager to do this now that he was installed on the couch, and he yawned widely and said: "God, I'm tired."

Karen poured him a cup of coffee and put it into his hand. She noticed he was wearing a dinner-jacket under his overcoat and she said:

"I thought this was mighty early for someone like you. Haven't you been to bed, or is that a leading question?"

Simon smiled sardonically. "Dear little Karen," he remarked dryly. "I've been playing poker, that's all. I admit I haven't spent the night between silken sheets and on a luxuriously sprung mattress, but on the other hand, I haven't been indulging in debauchery. Sorry to disappoint you, darling."

Karen lit a cigarette and moved away from him.

"Tell me, Karen," he said suddenly, "why don't I

attract you, when brother Paul used to send you into raptures?"

Karen flushed. "Do you really want to know?" she asked, turning round slowly.

"But of course. I imagine there's a reason."

"Oh yes, Simon. There's a reason. I simply think you're a weak-kneed, unintelligent oaf, with little else but sex inside your empty head. Does that satisfy you?"

Simon had the grace to flush deeply, and finishing his coffee he replaced his cup on the tray.

"Well, I did provoke that, I suppose," he said, with an attempt at light-heartedness that annoyed Karen anew. How could he sit there and allow her to speak to him in that manner? Had he no feelings? No pride?

She sighed again. "Well, Simon, you've had your coffee. Now perhaps, after all this, you can tell me what goes on."

"After what you've said, I feel that my journey was a wasted effort," he replied, sighing to himself. "I secretly thought you really liked me, even if I did rate second to Paul."

Karen shrugged. "Well, now you know. Why are you here? Is it about Sandra?"

"Yes," Simon nodded. "She and I have been having a good time together."

"I can imagine," exclaimed Karen. "She ought to have more sense. And so ought you."

"But darling! Paul has told me to lay off Sandra, and I hoped you might be able to dissuade him. After all, I've not harmed Sandra."

"You must be joking," she cried, half amused at his inflated ego. "Good heavens, Simon, it was I who asked Paul to intercede in the first place. My mother nearly had hysterics when she found out who Sandra was dating."

Simon looked at her with distaste. "Karen! Do you mean to tell me that you're behind all this?"

"I, and my mother," she replied coolly. "Why? Simon, you just aren't a fit escort for any woman! Apart from Julia, that is. You're married, remember!"

Simon frowned. "That's our affair," he retorted, irritated.

"Well, did you really believe that I would encourage a liaison between my sister and a married man, any married man?" exclaimed Karen. "And a man like you has the worst possible influence on her. She's wild enough as it is, without you encouraging her in your crazy fashion."

"Indeed? Thank you, Miss Stacey," he muttered, angry now. "But I don't think you realize just how infatuated Sandra is. You won't separate her from me so easily. Oh, Paul thinks he's got the upper hand, but it's not that simple."

"What do you mean?" Karen asked anxiously. Surely there were not going to be repercussions in this sordid affair?

Suddenly there was a knock at the door. Karen frowned, and Simon raised his eyebrows.

"More visitors?" he remarked sarcastically. "I wonder who this can be?"

Karen shrugged and stubbing out her cigarette she walked to the door and opened it. Paul stood on the threshold, tall and immaculate in a dark blue suit, with a dark blue fitted tie and sparkling white shirt. His immaculate appearance showed Simon's rather haggard appearance to disadvantage, and Karen could not help but think that Paul always looked better dressed than anyone else, no matter what he wore.

But Paul's face was cold and his eyes looked past Karen to the man lounging on her settee. The dark eyes were unfathomable and Karen felt her nerves jumping at the unpleasant expression on his face.

"Well, well," Paul drawled at length. "You are popular today, or should I say notorious?"

His cold eyes surveyed Karen's state of *déshabille* and make-up-less face, and she knew immediately what he was thinking.

She clasped her fingers. "What a surprise ..." she began awkwardly.

"I'm sure it must be," remarked Paul sardonically. "If I'd known you knew Simon so intimately ... shall we say, I'd have let you plead with him yourself. As it was, I believed you were too fastidious to bother with a man like him."

"I was – I am – I mean, you surely don't believe he's here because I invited him?" she exclaimed desperately.

"It certainly looks as though he's at home here," replied Paul coldly. "Perhaps you wanted Sandra to stop seeing him so that you would have no competition."

Simon decided it was time to intervene. He rose to his feet.

"Much as it goes against my better judgment," he said, slowly and deliberately, "I feel I must say that Karen is not interested in me. She has said so in no uncertain terms, I may add."

"Thank you," said Karen, sighing with relief, but Paul's face did not change. He shrugged, and said:

"Well, anyway, Karen, I'm sure you will have been told that I've already spoken to Simon and he has ... agreed ... to stop seeing Sandra. Anyway, Simon, it would hardly be worthwhile, bothering with two of them. I'm sure you would find Karen just as delectable for your needs ..."

Karen's hand moved to slap his face as her anger exploded into action, but he was too quick for her and his fingers closed round her wrist like a vice.

"I think not," he murmured softly and cruelly. His eyes narrowed as he looked down into her pale, oval face. "Poor misunderstood Karen," he continued, "you'll never learn, will you, darling?"

"Let go of me!" she exclaimed, between her teeth.

"My pleasure," he said releasing her wrist immediately. "Good-bye, Karen. I don't suppose we'll be meeting again."

He turned and walked away towards the lift and

Karen stood and watched him, rubbing her sore wrist. She was absolutely furious and she turned round on Simon when Paul disappeared into the lift.

"Now see what you've done!" she spat at him. "You Frazers! You think you rule the earth!"

Simon's eyes widened. "Hey, come on now!" he exclaimed. "I didn't stir up that tornado. Don't go blaming me. I agree Paul wasn't strictly pleased to see me here, but that's nothing. After all, he's nothing to you or you to him. What are you getting so het up about?"

"Get out!" exclaimed Karen holding back the hot tears that were pricking her eyes with a great physical effort.

"Okay, honey, but remember what I said, won't you?"

Simon strode out of the door. "Do you think brother Paul might give me a lift to the office if I asked him?"

Karen slammed the door without replying and leaned against it feeling sick. The morning had turned out so badly already and it was barely eleven o'clock.

She walked into her bedroom to get dressed, allowing the hot tears to flow unheeded down her cheeks. She had no opportunity to speak to Paul about what Simon had said about Sandra, and it didn't look as though she was to be given the chance now.

Why, oh, why had Paul chosen that particular morning to come? As for Simon, his colossal conceit had convinced him that whatever her attitude, Karen was really quite fond of him – sufficiently so at any rate to watch him ruin her sister's life without raising a finger to prevent it. She sighed heavily. Life was suddenly so complicated.

Paul had lunch alone at a small restaurant near the Frazer building. He felt unreasonably depressed and physically disturbed. Food was anathema to him and he had three cups of coffee and a cigar instead of his usual three-course meal. Seeing his brother at Karen's apartment that morning had flung his whole being into chaotic disorder and he inwardly cursed himself for going there. He also cursed himself for being stupid enough to feel anything about the affair at all. The only reason he had gone to the apartment in the first place was to speak to Karen privately about his talk with Simon, and he had been astounded to find his brother there. Just why was he there, anyway? Could they possibly have been lying and were really lovers? Simon had not slept at home, that was obvious from his attire, and Karen had been wearing a housecoat. The thoughts tortured his aching mind and he stared moodily down at his cigar.

If Karen were to start an affair with Simon, taunted his thoughts again, what would he do then? Could he stand it? And if not, why? Seeing her had brought all this upon him and he wished to God he had never met her again. His whole carefully constructed life seemed to be shifting on sands; emotional sands. He even considered the thought of having an affair with her himself, if she was agreeable, simply to get her out of his system. It was simply sex raising its ugly head once more. He shook his head. Why should he even consider having an affair with Karen at all? He had Ruth, and no doubt she would be willing to console him if he so desired. What was it about Karen that seemed to get under his very skin? There was only one answer; sex appeal.

He finished his last cup of coffee and was about to rise when a young voice said lightly:

"Hello, Paul. What a surprise. May I join you?"

"Sandra!" he exclaimed, standing up. The sight of Karen's sister startled him. After his deep thoughts he felt sure something of his feelings must show in his face.

Sandra Stacey was not a bit like Karen. She was much smaller for one thing and quite plump, with full breasts and broad thighs and a youthful disregard for fashion. Her fair hair hung limply on either side of her oval face, longer than Karen's but not so well groomed. She was dressed in a dark blue duffel coat with a hood and long off-white tights which ended in thick-heeled shoes. At her age Karen had been tall and slim with good dress sense, even if her clothes like Sandra's had never been expensive. Sandra's face was slightly freckled, a fact that she abhorred.

"Nice to see you," she remarked, and seated herself so that Paul was forced to sit down too.

"I'm afraid I was just leaving," he said politely. "I didn't know you frequented this place." It seemed an expensive eating house for her.

"I don't normally," she replied, smiling confidently. "But I work in a hairdressers near here – I'm a trainee stylist, you know – and Simon is taking me to lunch. You may as well know, because he may turn up at any moment."

Paul thought this was highly unlikely in the circumstances, but he did not reply. He had no intention of breaking Simon's bad news for him. Sandra would find out soon enough.

"Then can't I order you anything?" he asked slowly.

"Oh, no, thanks. I'll wait. How are you? It's so long since Mother and I have seen you. You've quite deserted us."

Paul shrugged and offered her a cigarette. "Yes, I'm afraid I find life pretty hectic."

"I'll bet! You've just got engaged, haven't you? I saw it in *The Times*. My boss reads it, you know."

Paul smiled and rose to his feet. He was not in the mood for conversation.

"I must go," he said apologetically.

"That's all right, Paul, I understand. Simon is a busy man too. He's always having to rush back to the office." She flushed. "Tell me, Paul, do you disapprove of our relationship?"

Paul bit his lip. "You're a trifle young for him," he said dryly. "Besides, Sandra, Simon is a married man. What about his wife? Don't you care about Julia?"

"You should know what kind of a person she is," said Sandra with youthful candour. "Anyway, Simon will look after me, whatever happens."

"I doubt it," remarked Paul. "Simon's not the constant type. Look around. However, even if he was an angel in disguise, he's still a married man."

He fastened his coat and wondered how much of this conversation was really going in. Sandra seemed too bemused by Simon to care what he was, or did.

"But he was very young when he got married," said Sandra. "And he's only thirteen years older than me." She flushed. "Karen is twelve years younger than you."

"And Karen was much older than you at eighteen," replied Paul coolly. "I'm sorry, Sandra, but there it is."

"I get sick of hearing that," exclaimed Sandra hotly. "How could she be?"

Paul shrugged. How could he explain that Karen was born older than Sandra, somehow?

"I really must go," he said, glancing at his watch. "Au revoir."

"Cheerio, Paul. I'll give Karen your love," she giggled slightly, but Paul merely half smiled and walked away.

CHAPTER THREE

DURING Thursday Karen telephoned her mother and told her she had had confirmation from Paul that he had spoken to Simon. She did not give any details of their meetings although Madeline tried her hardest to find out what had happened. Karen remained aloof with her and Madeline had to be content that Karen had done her best.

She was highly delighted that Sandra was no longer involved with "that dreadful man", and was convinced that Sandra would eventually turn to her for comfort. After all she was her mother, and Sandra didn't know she had asked Karen to intervene. Karen wondered bleakly if there was a showdown, whether Madeline would admit to having had anything to do with the affair at all. Madeline needed to feel wanted, and if Sandra found out she had instituted such a cruel deed she might well turn against her mother. Karen sighed. As she and Sandra had so little in common anyway, it did not really matter what Sandra thought of her, Karen.

It would indeed be a tragedy for Madeline if Sandra began to show independent tendencies, more reminiscent of Karen. She had never condoned Karen's actions in almost anything. Sandra was her baby, her protégée, and she had always clung to her for that reason.

After Karen had rung off she lit a cigarette and went to make herself some coffee before starting work. It was already late in the afternoon and if she didn't start soon it would be another day wasted. But, just at the moment, her work had lost its charm and instead she found her thoughts wandering back to Paul and his fiancée.

The following evening Karen dressed with care for the ball at the Magnifique. She bathed, long and luxuriously, and took a long while dressing, taking everything in slow precision. She had bought herself a new evening dress just that morning, and she wanted to look sleek and glamorous for once. Too long she had shut herself away from society. Life could not go on like that. She was young and unattached. It was only common sense that she should do something about it.

The dress, when she slipped it on, clung to her body, moulding her rich curves, accentuating her tender waist. It was made of black velvet, with a high round neckline, and tight sleeves. It was a long time since she had spent so much money on herself. Her only adornment was a pair of drop diamond earrings, sparkling circles that winked as she moved her head.

She wore a white sable stole which had been an anniversary gift from Paul, and her hair hung loose and straight to her shoulders. Its paleness accentuated the darkness of her dress, caressing her cheeks, and framing her attractive features. For a moment she regretted dressing like this for Lewis. After all, he was pressing enough as it was in his desire to make her his wife. He might think she was deliberately setting out to attract him. She sighed. It was too late now anyway. She had no time to change and he would be here at any moment. She took a last look at herself in the mirror and then went to pour the cocktails before Lewis arrived.

At the back of her mind there was a sudden sadness as she thought of Paul. Would he have admired her dress? She half wished he could see her if only to prove she was not pining away for love of him. She would like to think there was still an element of regret about their divorce. But this was a very faint hope; he probably found Ruth equally beautiful, and she would be quite happy to be his wife and not make the demands on him that Karen had done.

A knock came at her door and she went to open it. Lewis stood there looking elegant in evening clothes. His eyes were eloquent with admiration. Karen invited him in for a drink before they left and he accepted eagerly.

But Karen did not waste too much time. Now that Lewis was here she was eager to be gone. To start this evening which she suddenly felt was going to be a flop. Lewis was not Paul, and it was no good wishing he was.

They had dinner in the restaurant of the Magnifique. Lewis had reserved a table and the meal was delicious. The Magnifique was quite a newly built hotel, and its clientele were all rich and quite often famous too. Karen found herself identifying stars of television and films and in her interest she forgot her earlier depression. Realizing suddenly that Lewis was addressing her, she said:

"I'm sorry, Lewis, I was miles away."

He smiled. "I was merely saying what a beautiful young woman you are, my dear."

"Thank you, kind sir," she replied lightly. "I'm glad you approve. I wondered whether I ought to have accepted you really. You're far too patient with me, Lewis. Why don't you find yourself a wife? I'll never change, you know."

His eyes narrowed only slightly, and then he said:

"We'll see. My housekeeper is leaving at the end of next month. Her sister in Glasgow has been in hospital and she has promised to go and look after her when she comes home. It looks like being a very long job. I don't suppose you would care to take on her position?"

"As your housekeeper?" asked Karen teasingly.

"As my wife," Lewis said determinedly.

Karen shook her head. "Isn't that Jane Mannering over there?" she asked evasively. "She looks much younger than she does on the screen."

Lewis shrugged his slim shoulders. "You're an adept, aren't you, Karen?" he asked.

"At what?" she queried coolly.

Lewis frowned. "You know what I mean," he answered heavily. "But we won't mention it again, as it seems to annoy you."

Karen flushed and for a while they ate in silence.

When the meal was over and they were having liqueurs

with their coffee, Lewis said:

"Tell me, has this business over Sandra been satisfactorily settled?"

"You might say that," replied Karen, managing a small smile. "We must wait and see, mustn't we?"

"As in all things," he replied enigmatically.

When dinner was over they joined the crowds of people arriving for the ball, which began at ten-thirty. Karen and Lewis sat in the cocktail bar until after eleven, and Karen found the unusual amount of alcohol she was consuming was relaxing her, and she began to enjoy herself. Before they entered the ballroom she went into the cloakroom to powder her nose. It was thronged with the most elaborately-clad women, emeralds, sapphires, rubies and diamonds, all competing with each other in their magnificence.

Karen repaired her make-up and applied a coral lipstick to her lips. Her long lashes required no mascara and she wore only a little eye-shadow. The smooth silkiness of her hair looked infinitely more attractive than the complicated coiffures of the women around her.

She rejoined Lewis at the arched entrance to the massive ballroom. He was standing watching the dancers, smoking a cigarette.

"Ah, you're ready," he said, as she joined him. "There's quite a crowd here as you can see. Let's try and find a table."

"All right, Lewis. I'm really enjoying myself. I'm so glad you invited me."

"The pleasure is all mine," returned Lewis suavely, and they strolled into the crowds thronging the dance floor.

There were tables set around the polished sprung floor, each with a lamp in its centre emitting an intimate glow. The orchestra, a famous one, was installed on a low dais at the far end of the hall while at the other end a long bar had been erected. The rest of the walls were set with tall mirrors which reflected the dancers many times over.

The ceiling was high and arched and fluted pillars supported its carved elegance.

"It's very impressive," said Karen looking about her with interest. "I had no idea it would be like this."

Lewis smiled, satisfied that he had pleased her.

They found a vacant table and Lewis ordered drinks from a passing waiter. There seemed to be plenty of waiters passing amongst the guests and everyone seemed relaxed and informal.

After watching the progress of the dancers for a while, Lewis said: "Shall we dance, or do you prefer to watch?"

"Oh, no, I prefer to dance," exclaimed Karen, smiling, "Let's, please, Lewis. My feet are positively itching!"

Lewis smiled and helped her up from the table. He swung her round into the rhythm of the music. It was so nice to feel as though she was living again and Karen found she could follow Lewis's lead with an ease which surprised her, for it was so long since she had danced. He was quite a good dancer and they danced three times without a break.

The band suddenly struck up a cha-cha, and Karen looked teasingly at Lewis. "Can you?" she asked, smiling.

"I can but try," he replied, smiling too, and they contrived to follow the rhythm without much success. Lewis was not a born dancer and Karen could not follow his rather jerky movements. They were laughing together when Karen's attention was drawn to four people entering the ballroom. They were endeavouring to reach a table near the orchestra and were threading their way among the crowds of people thronging the edge of the floor. There were two men and two women. One of the men was Paul Frazer.

Lewis noticed her disturbed expression and said urgently:

"Is anything wrong, Karen? You look pale."

"Paul has just arrived," she replied, concentrating on

her feet. "He hasn't seen me, I don't think. He's with Ian Fellowes and his wife, and another woman who must be Ruth, I suppose."

Ian Fellowes was an old school friend of Paul's, and he and his wife had been frequent visitors at their house in the old days.

Lewis frowned angrily. "My God!" he exclaimed. "I've been to dozens of these charity affairs and he's never turned up before. Why has he decided to come tonight?"

"He wasn't engaged before," replied Karen, running a tongue over her suddenly dry lips. "Ruth probably persuaded him."

"Probably," Lewis nodded glumly. "Do you want to sit down?"

"Please." Karen felt like making herself as inconspicuous as possible. "I feel like a drink, just at the moment."

"Of course." They went back to their table which was fortunately across the hall from Paul Frazer's party. Karen was able to observe them when no one was dancing, without them being able to observe her. She sipped her gin and vermouth and accepted a cigarette from Lewis, allowing herself to look across at Ruth. She was curious to see what kind of woman Paul was going to make his second wife.

She saw Ruth was wearing an elaborate ball gown of pink satin, overlaid with lace. Small and vivacious, Karen could see she was very attractive. If Paul could dwarf Karen who was a tall girl, he would certainly be much taller than Ruth who was very petite and probably made him feel rather protective towards her.

The dancing began again and they were obscured from her view. She looked at Lewis and found he was watching her.

"So that's Ruth," she said lightly. "She's very pretty, isn't she?"

"I suppose so," remarked Lewis, frowning. "However,

I prefer blondes myself. She seems rather talkative."

They had both noticed how Ruth monopolized the conversation, and continually attempted to draw Paul's attention to her.

"You're biased," said Karen, with a smile, and she sighed.

Lewis swallowed his drink and signalled the waiter for two more. "I wonder what Sandra will do if she stops seeing Simon?" he said suddenly. "I think she needs a firm hand. Your mother should have married again."

"Oh, Paul used to control her," remarked Karen idly. "She adored him!"

Lewis's face hardened. "Then maybe I could do so too," he said.

Karen flushed. "I doubt it, Lewis." She looked into his lean pale face. She knew that Lewis had not the necessary power to control a teenager like Sandra. He had had no experience, for one thing. Paul had always controlled Simon in his youth and Sandra had obeyed Paul partially because of his dark good looks and magnetic attraction. He had charm, there was no denying it, and Sandra had fallen victim to that charm. She had imagined herself in love with him and had treated his every wish as her command. Lewis was not likely to appeal to her in that sense. And besides, Madeline did not like Lewis herself, whereas she too had doted on Paul.

Karen smiled at Lewis now and said: "Lewis darling, I think not. Sandra's hardly your type, or you hers, but she always thought she was in love with Paul. She used to trail after him like a lapdog. I don't think she ever saw anyone else."

"I see." Lewis was taken aback. The idea of Sandra imagining herself in love with Paul Frazer had never occurred to him. He found the idea distasteful.

Karen finished her cigarette and rose to her feet. "Excuse me a moment," she said. "I'm just going to the cloakroom. I shan't be long."

"All right." Lewis looked up at her and rose abruptly to his feet. "I'll wait here."

She smiled and slipped away between the tables, threading her way to the door, seeking the cool air of the hall. What she really needed more than anything else was air.

She fanned herself with her evening bag and wandered slowly along the corridor to the cloakroom. The hall was thickly carpeted, pillars supporting the roof here as in the ballroom. It was all very modern, but Karen liked it. She had almost reached the cloakroom when she saw Paul.

He was leaning negligently against one of the pillars, smoking a cigar and talking to another man. He looked big and broad and attractive in a dinner jacket, his tanned skin contrasting sharply with the brilliant whiteness of his dinner shirt.

Feeling a surge of excitement, Karen strolled towards them and her approach caused Paul to glance her way. His handsome face showed no surprise and she assumed he had seen her even before she had noticed him.

Looking at him she wondered why she had allowed Lewis to persuade her that a divorce from Paul was the best thing. Left alone, she would probably have gone back to him, and tonight that seemed a most desirable occurrence. Had he not divorced her, she knew she would never have divorced him, and she would still have been his wife. Now, as his eyes met hers, he looked so cool and aloof that she felt anger at his apparent complacency.

However, he straightened and dropped his cigar to the floor and ground his heel on it. He was obviously not going to ignore her and Karen felt unreasonably glad. His companion looked round too and saw her, and Karen saw it was no one she had ever been introduced to.

"Hello, Paul," she murmured, overwhelmingly pleased that she was looking her best in the new evening gown.

She had wanted Paul to see her and now she was getting her wish.

"Karen," he nodded, his eyes unfathomable. He turned to his companion, a man of about thirty-five, with fair, unruly hair, and a cheerful, carefree expression. Before he could introduce Karen, however, the man smiled jovially and said:

"Come on, Paul, won't you introduce me? You seem to know all the most delightful girls."

Paul half smiled, and Karen wondered what was going through his mind. Was he thinking that Ruth was twice as delightful as herself?

"Karen," he said, "this is Anthony Stoker – Sir Anthony – an old friend from my university days. Tony, this is Karen ... Stacey." He hesitated an infinitesimal moment over her surname as though he still thought of her as Karen Frazer.

"Hello," said Karen, smiling, and Tony shook her hand vigorously.

"How do you do?" he replied in return. His hand was large and calloused but perfectly manicured. Everything about him was big, in fact what he lacked in looks he made up for in personality. He seemed a warm-hearted, amiable man, and Karen took an immediate liking to him. He was not the kind of man to whom she could be attracted, but he would make a good friend, she thought.

"I'm fine," she replied politely. "Are you enjoying the ball?"

"Very much," replied Tony. "I helped to organize it, actually."

He smiled at them both beneficently and then suddenly exclaimed: "My God, Paul, the penny has just dropped. Is this – well, I mean – the girl who was your wife?"

Paul shrugged his broad shoulders. "She was my wife many moons ago," he said coolly, and Karen felt her cheeks burn.

"Heavens! Talk about fools rushing in, etc! Have I

made a complete ass of myself, Paul old boy?"

"Not at all," replied Paul easily. "Karen is a very attractive woman. She knows that already, I'm sure."

Karen's flush deepened. She hated being discussed as though she were not present. Breaking into their conversation she began: "Are you alone, Paul?"

"Actually, I'm waiting for Ruth," he replied, his eyes holding hers. "She's in the ladies' cloakroom, I believe."

"Oh, I see. I saw you arrive earlier."

"I know you did," remarked Paul calmly. "I saw you across the room when we sat at our table."

Karen shivered. She had been quite unaware that her observation had been returned. What had he thought? Had he thought her intensely curious?

"I see." She cast about in her mind for something to say. The conversation so far had been very uninspiring, and she wished she could think of something witty to say to make them laugh.

"By the way," she murmured at last, looking up at him through the long veil of her lashes, "thank you for speaking to Simon."

Paul looked slightly uncomfortable, as she had intended he should. Tony looked on, obviously immensely intrigued at this turn of events.

"I didn't have a chance to thank you properly, yesterday," she continued determinedly.

"That's all right," replied Paul stiffly, while his eyes sparkled dangerously, daring her to say anything more.

Karen looked at Tony. "Don't mind us," she murmured, smiling. "Paul and I are still good friends, aren't we, darling? After all, we're civilized people, aren't we? Not primitives. We're able to be quite natural with each other. Aren't I right, Paul?"

"Perfectly," replied Paul coldly, but his eyes were positively glittering with menace now.

Tony broke the unarmed combat by saying:

"How about returning to the ballroom with me, then, Karen? I'd like to dance with you, if I may."

Paul stiffened at Tony's words. Karen was conscious that for some reason, Paul did not wish her to dance with Tony. Could he be jealous? No, that was ridiculous. He probably didn't want a friend of his associating with a woman like her, or rather like he supposed her to be.

Ignoring his attitude, however, she replied: "Thank you, Tony. I'd like that, very much."

"Good." Tony looked back at Paul. "See you later then, old boy."

"Of course," Paul was aloof and Karen knew she had disturbed him, but whether seriously or not she could not know.

Tony took her hand and they returned to the ballroom. He turned out to be a good dancer for all his bulk, and was an amusing companion. He explained that he himself had invited Paul and his friends to this ball as his guests, and that his own partner had let him down at the last minute.

He joked about his title, which he did not take very seriously, and told her he farmed an estate in Wiltshire, that had been in the Stoker family for generations. They were not rich, for all their money was ploughed back into the land. That explained his calloused hands, and Karen admired him for sticking it out and not giving up. Had he sold the estate, he and his mother and sister could have lived in London in comparative luxury, but they loved the soil and preferred to live in Wiltshire and support their tenants.

From his description, the estate sounded delightful, and his family seemed genuine country folk, even if they were the local lords of the manor. His father was dead, he told her, and he and his mother and sister lived in a rambling old manor house overlooking the downs. Although he had known Paul since their Oxford days they had only met again recently and renewed their acquaintanceship. They has had lunch together a couple of times, and Tony had met Paul's American fiancée.

Karen let him ramble on. She was vaguely interested,

but her mind kept harking back to Paul. It was good to listen to his chatter while half of her mind was elsewhere. He was an undemanding partner and she followed him easily without any thought.

Once she caught sight of Lewis and felt her conscience prick her. He looked strained and almost angry about something, and when he saw her too and she waved, he merely frowned and ignored her. She felt worried and very guilty, and when the dance ended she explained that she was with her employer and that he was waiting for her.

"Oh, I say, really?" exclaimed Tony. "Well, do you think I might join you for a while? I feel rather a gooseberry with Paul, you know."

Karen's lips tightened, but she said: "Of course. Lewis and I are old friends. He won't object, I'm sure."

"Oh, good," said Tony warmly. "I'd like the opportunity of another dance later, if I may."

Karen smiled up at him and allowed him to retain hold of her hand as they returned to the table where Lewis was seated. He rose abruptly to his feet at their approach, and as he wasn't a tall man, Tony dwarfed him both in height and bulk.

"Where the devil have you been all this time, Karen?" exclaimed Lewis in a cold and angry voice. "And who is this?"

"The name is Stoker, Anthony Stoker," said Tony at once, not liking the other man's tone or manner. "Who might you be?"

"Oh, please," exclaimed Karen awkwardly, not understanding Lewis's grim face. "Lewis, this is Tony, Tony, this is Lewis Martin, my employer."

The two men shook hands with ill grace and Karen half wished she had left Tony behind.

"Tony was in the hall talking to Paul when I went to the cloakroom," she explained. "Paul introduced us."

"You mean Frazer again, I suppose," said Lewis frowning.

"Of course."

"I see," Lewis looked at Karen, "And now perhaps you'll dance with me, Karen."

"Of course," she said again, bewildered by Lewis's possessive jealousy. She had never given him any reason to suppose they were anything more than good friends for all his talk of marriage, and she didn't like to feel possessed like this. After all, he had no hold on her. She was a free woman.

They danced for a while in silence, and then he said in a strained voice:

"I suppose I ought to apologize. I'm behaving boorishly."

"Yes, you are," agreed Karen hotly, glad he had brought it out into the open. "What on earth is wrong with you? I've only been away fifteen minutes."

"I know, I know. I'm sorry." Lewis sighed heavily. "It must be patently obvious that I'm madly jealous. You wouldn't know what that feels like, would you? Wanting someone so badly and knowing they don't want you."

Karen flushed. "Lewis . . . not now . . . not again . . ."

Lewis flushed too. "I know," he muttered. "Don't say it again. Just don't flaunt young men in my face like this. I can't help my feelings. I've come to the conclusion that you must be naturally frigid."

"Frigid!" Karen almost laughed. The way even speaking to Paul caused the heat to flood her body; and Lewis thought she was frigid. She shivered. "Maybe you're right," she said at length, deciding to take the easiest way out.

"I'm convinced of it," replied Lewis slowly, and looked searchingly at her. "But one day you'll need a man again, Karen, and I intend to be around when that happens."

Karen frowned at this, and did not reply. Lewis's attitude was strange tonight to say the least and she presumed he must have been drinking too heavily all evening.

Back at the table, Tony lounged in a chair, waiting for

them. He looked pleased to see Karen and got up swiftly and held her chair for her as she sat down. He really was good company, she mused, and he took her mind off Paul and Lewis for a while. She had even got around to thinking of Lewis as a problem now. Surely she was not going to have to change her job after all this time? But if Lewis became really impossible, something would have to be done. She couldn't have him going around monopolizing her and spoiling her life.

She eventually got through the evening by dancing alternately with Tony and Lewis, but she found she now enjoyed the dances with Tony best. He was entertaining and asked for nothing in return, and his enjoyment of her company was simply because his own partner had not been able to come, and there were no strings attached.

Lewis was definitely not his usual self. He held her too tightly for her liking and she wondered if he was used to drinking as much as he had done. He breathed down her neck heavily and she felt stifled. She really thought he was having to hold his emotions in check by a severe effort, and she could only assume that Paul's presence was in some way responsible. She had never seen him like this before and she began to realize she did not know him as well as she had thought.

Ian Fellowes worked for Paul in the Frazer building. He was a chief sales representative, and a good man at his job. He and Paul had been friends for a very long time and the difference in their status had never come between them.

Margaret Fellowes was twenty-eight, the same age as Ruth. She and Ruth got along quite well together, although as Margaret had known and liked Karen she refused to discuss Paul's first wife with his proposed second. This infuriated Ruth, who was by now avid for information about the first Mrs. Frazer. She had never even seen a picture of Karen. There were none about Paul's apartment, and although this pleased her she would have liked to have known what Karen was like. She felt almost as though she had an invisible enemy.

Tonight, they had a table near the orchestra and they had all danced quite a lot. Ruth was not keen to dance with Ian, but when he asked her she did not like to refuse every time; but it meant that Margaret danced with Paul, and although it was ridiculous, jealousy consumed her at these times.

She was pleased with her dress with its layer of lace over satin. It was just the thing to complement her pink and white colouring and she felt sure Paul admired it, even though he rarely commented on her clothes. Margaret's dress was grey crepe and in Ruth's opinion it had seen better days. She felt quite sure that she was far more attractive in Ian's eyes too, but Paul showed no signs of jealousy. It was annoying really because she would have liked to have aroused Paul in that way, but these last few days since his lunch with Karen he had become cool and aloof, and she couldn't understand it. Ruth was not used to being denied anything. Her parents had spoiled her terribly and indulged her every whim.

She sat now running her fingers along Paul's immaculately clad arm, wondering what she could say to attract his attention. He seemed to be miles away, in spirit if not in fact. Earlier, he and Ian had been discussing some new textile they were manufacturing and she had been absolutely bored. She really wasn't getting enough attention tonight.

Suddenly she noticed that a crowd of people were gathering around a couple who were dancing in the centre of the floor. The band was playing beat music and Ruth supposed somebody was making an exhibition of themselves. It might be interesting and amusing to watch them.

"Come on, Paul," she said, tugging at his arm. "Let's go and watch!"

The Fellowes were already dancing, so Paul reluctantly rose and allowed himself to be drawn across the floor to the group in the centre. There were no other couples dancing now, everyone was watching. Paul halted abruptly in his tracks. The two people who were gyrating laughingly to the music were Tony Stoker and . . . Karen.

He felt the blood pounding through his veins as he watched them, and was infuriated with his traitorous body. God, he had to get control of himself!

"Why, it's Tony Stoker," exclaimed Ruth. "Aren't they good? Not that I would make an exhibition of myself like that."

Paul did not reply and she looked up at him. His face was dark and inscrutable and she frowned.

"Whatever is wrong?" she asked irritably. "Didn't you want to come and see?"

"Not particularly," replied Paul grimly.

"Why?" And then Ruth had a sudden insight. It was something in Paul's face, something about his expression that made her say suddenly and accusingly: "You know that girl, don't you? Who is she?"

"What makes you think that?" evaded Paul slowly.

"I just feel it. Does she work in your office? Is she your assistant or something?"

"She used to work for me," he replied quietly. "That's Karen, Ruth."

Ruth's face was a picture of incredulity.

"Karen ... not *the* Karen?" she exclaimed.

"The same," remarked Paul, thrusting his hands into his trouser pockets. "Now, are you satisfied? Does that please you?"

"But I don't understand," she began, "I imagined she was your age. Paul, you never told me she was so young."

"You never asked me," he replied coolly. "Karen is twenty-five now. Three years younger than you, I believe."

Ruth flushed angrily. How she wished she had not suggested coming to watch the dancers. How was she to know that it might be Karen? She had not even known she was here, and yet Paul had not seemed surprised. Had he known she was to be here? Questions flew wildly round in her mind and then she quelled them. It was stupid thinking in this way. After all, they had been married and divorced. They were nothing to each other now. The very fact that they could talk together normally proved there was no feeling left.

And yet as Ruth watched Karen she felt suddenly furious. Karen was a very beautiful woman, not the old hag she had imagined, or the hard-faced creature who flaunted herself shamelessly before men and acted younger than her years. Mentally calculating, she realized that Karen could only have been eighteen when she married Paul, and this appalled her. After all, they had known one another so intimately at that time, while she at eighteen was still attending college and making casual dates with boys. Certainly nothing more serious than that. Paul, a man of thirty, had found this creature mentally and physically satisfying at that time, when Ruth herself would have been tongue-tied with a man of his age.

The girl, for she looked little more, had shared three years of Paul's life, long before she had even met him, and the thought sickened her. She wanted to feel the most beautiful woman in his life, but now was she to think of this girl every time he touched her, wondering what he still felt for her?

Her thoughts frightened her. Life had seemed so simple and uncomplicated before this week, with the June wedding so much nearer and the thoughts of their honeymoon uppermost in her mind.

Now everything had changed, and all because this girl's stupid sister had to go and get herself involved with Paul's married brother. It was unbearable. She felt she wanted to stand and scream and cry and get her own way as she had done in years gone by. She wanted to stamp her feet and if possible, stamp them on this woman who had come back into Paul's life, whether he was aware of it or not. But she had to act naturally. Whatever had happened was in the past and Paul was hers now. If she showed she was afraid of the power of this woman, who knew what might happen? No, she had got to act as usual and be the loving and understanding fiancée. After they were married; well, that would be a different story.

"Let's go, shall we, darling?" she murmured softly, sliding her hand through Paul's arm. "Paul, let's go back to the hotel."

Paul was quite willing to oblige her. He felt like leaving himself. He didn't particularly want company, he would have preferred to be alone with his churning emotions. He needed a drink. A good drink!

"All right," he said, with apparent indifference. "If that's what you want. I thought you were enjoying yourself."

"I was . . . that is, I've developed rather a headache," replied Ruth swiftly. "I just feel like relaxing in the peace and quiet of my suite, that's all."

"Right." Paul nodded and turned around, away from the watching throng around Karen and Tony. "We must let Ian and Margaret know we're going."

Ruth's suite at the Dorchester was the height of luxury, and was costing her father an enormous amount of money every day. But Hiram Delaney counted his bank-notes in thousands, not tens, and consequently the cost of installing his daughter in a fashionable hotel in London was merely a pin-prick in his bank balance.

The lounge of the suite was deserted. Ruth's personal maid had been given the night off, and Ruth flung herself with careless abandon on a low divan. Paul loosened his dark, fur-collared overcoat, and walked round like a caged panther. He was wondering how soon he could get away.

Ruth held out a hand to him. "Come and sit down, darling, and take off your coat," she said lazily. "You're not going yet, are you?"

Paul bit his lip. "I was under the impression that you had a headache," he replied slowly. "You seem to have recovered remarkably quickly."

Ruth flushed. "The fresh air has helped," she replied defensively.

"Nevertheless as it is quite late, I think I'll go," said Paul firmly. "You get to bed and rest and I'll see you in the morning, hmm?"

He bent and kissed her cheek, but she wrapped her arms round his neck and pulled him down to her. "Don't be so aloof," she whispered, confident that she could dispel the mood he seemed to be in. She put her lips to his, urging him to take her in his arms and make love to her.

But Paul resisted, and after a moment she was forced to release him and allow him to get up. She was flushed and uncomfortable. He had never repulsed her before. It was embarrassing and degrading and she felt angry. But controlling her feelings, she said: "Will you meet me for lunch tomorrow?"

Paul shrugged. "Ring me in the morning, honey. I'll try and make it."

"Thank you," she said, the sarcasm only slightly veiled, and with a half smile he left her.

After he had gone Ruth rose from the couch. She had not got a headache at all and her plans to get Paul to herself had gone sadly awry. She unzipped her dress with careless fingers and catching the material in the clasp she ripped it open, tearing it from bodice to waist. Angrily, she tore off the ruined garment and flung it to the floor. As she pushed open the door of her bedroom she found her hands were trembling and tears stung her eyes. Here she was; one of the richest young women in London, and she was going to bed soon after midnight in the most vicious of tempers.

Paul left the hotel and climbed into his car. Once inside he lit a cigarette before turning on the engine. Then he steered the sleek automobile along Park Lane, turning into Grosvenor Place and from there into the King's Road. He drove swiftly through the artists' quarter and on to the main road to Guildford.

His apartment was in Belgravia, but he had no desire for his bed just yet. Just beyond the suburbs he turned on to a back road which led into Richmond by a roundabout route. It was a very black night, but he could find his way here blindfolded, he thought wearily.

Just outside Richmond he turned into a private road which climbed steeply to a high brick wall in which were set a pair of wrought-iron gates, carved intricately with the name "Trevayne".

This was the house he had bought on his marriage to Karen. He had never sold it.

He turned into the driveway and curved up amongst the sentinel poplars to the wide, gravel forecourt before the low steps which led up to the double white doors. Tonight, in the darkness, the elegant beauty of the place could not be appreciated, but Paul knew what a gracious old building it was. Inside, of course, it had been extensively modernized, but the outside retained the aura of latter years.

The headlights of Paul's car swept the terrace before coming to rest and he stopped the engine, turning off the ignition. He slid out from behind the wheel and slammed the car door. The sound of the metal rang eerily in the night air, and Paul thrust his hands into his pockets and approached the terrace.

Ruth was unaware that Trevayne existed. He had never told anyone, not even his mother, that he still owned the house, everyone had assumed he had sold it and he was quite willing to let them go on thinking this. He had dismissed all the staff but the housekeeper and her husband when he divorced Karen, and Mr. and Mrs. Benson remained on in the empty building, keeping everything in readiness for if he ever chose to visit them. He had not been there at all since his engagement to Ruth; until now he had not felt the need to come.

Before he reached the front doors, the carriage light above the door was illuminated and a moment later Benson himself opened the door. Light streamed out on to the drive, enveloping Paul in its brightness.

Benson was in his dressing-gown, but he smiled broadly as he recognized his master.

"Why, Mr. Paul," he exclaimed. "This is a surprise. It must be three months since we've seen you."

Paul crossed the terrace and passed Benson, entering the wide entrance hall. The floor was polished mosaic of many colours and a huge oak chest gleamed from many polishings and was set with a huge vase containing spring flowers, at the foot of the fan-shaped staircase. The staircase was carpeted in gold and russet, brilliantly accentuating the dark panelling that mounted beside it.

"Yes, Benson. I'm sorry if I disturbed you. It's extremely late, I know."

"Oh, that's all right, sir," said Benson understandingly, although, Paul mused, he couldn't have any idea why Paul had turned up so late.

Benson closed the doors and locked them and then said:

"Will you be staying the night, sir?"

Paul nodded, removing his overcoat. "Yes, Benson, I will. I expect my bed is made up as usual."

"It is, sir. Maggie was only saying today that you might be calling on us in the near future. She's always prepared, if I may say so."

Paul smiled rather cynically and crossed the hall. "Is she in bed?"

"Yes, sir. Is there anything I can get you? Are you needing a meal?"

Paul shook his head and opened the door of the library. "No, not as long as there's plenty of Scotch."

"I put a new bottle in there today," said Benson immediately. "Are you sure that's all you need?"

"Positive," replied Paul abruptly. " 'Night, Benson. See you in the morning." He closed the library door and leaned back against it. Sanctuary!

The room was well lined with books, but in addition a small baby grand piano stood in one corner. He and Karen had used the room as a music-room and had spent many happy evenings alone in here. Paul could play the piano quite well and he had played all Karen's favourites like Chopin and Grieg.

He crossed to the tray of drinks standing near the piano on a low table, and helped himself to a stiff whisky. Swallowing the drink, he poured another and seated himself at the piano.

His fingers strayed over the keys, picking out the strains of *Clair de Lune*. It was a plaintive melody and as he looked towards the deep armchair by the fireplace he seemed to see Karen curled up on the chair watching him.

With a groan, he slammed down the lid, covering the keys, and lifted his drink. Then he stood up and loosened his collar, wandering about the room aimlessly. What in God's name was wrong with him now? Was he a man or a mouse? He cursed Simon for causing his dilemma in the first place. If he had never seen Karen he would never have felt any differently towards her and there was little chance that they would have ever met. They moved in different social circles. For a time, Karen had joined his sphere, but now she had returned to her own orbit. After all, most of the people he mixed with were very rich and very powerful. Financiers, bank owners, businessmen all of them, interested only in ways to make more money.

But he had seen Karen now and he knew he was still physically attracted to her. He did not deceive himself, Karen had always affected him this way. He had forgotten just how desirable she was.

To begin with he had always assumed she would marry Lewis, and so the idea of any other man having anything to do with her had not been his concern. But she was still free and unattached, and seeing her tonight dancing with Tony Stoker had positively shocked him. Tony had apparently been enchanted by her and even now was probably with her, either taking her home or at her apartment. Would he be allowed to kiss her? Hold her? Make love to her?

Paul felt the knife turn in his stomach. Blind jealousy was a ridiculous thing, but he knew he was feeling it. He felt like ringing her apartment to find out for himself, but pride held him back. What could he say? That he was checking up on her?

He reached for the bottle of whisky and filled his glass. He flung himself into an armchair still holding the bottle in his hand. It was going to be a long night . . .

CHAPTER FOUR

In actual fact Lewis took Karen home. Karen knew that Tony was quite willing to do so, but she felt that as she had come with Lewis it was her duty to go home with him. She would have preferred the uncomplicated company of Tony with Lewis in this frame of mind, but she decided she had nothing to be ashamed of and certainly she did not owe Lewis anything. His attitude was simply annoying.

Karen had seen Paul leave with Ruth. She had seen them talking to the Fellowes beforehand, and had later seen them going out of the archway. As they did not reappear at their table she assumed they must indeed have left.

She felt that after Paul's departure the evening had lost its charm. Why, she couldn't imagine; for he had not even danced with her, and their conversation had simply been a baiting match. Probably that was her fault for she did find delight in annoying him; in disturbing his apparent composure and assurance.

The only excuse for their early departure that she could see was that they wanted to be alone together. The idea frightened her by the tortuous emotions it aroused. After all, they were at liberty to do as they pleased and soon they would be married and together all the time. They probably spent hours and hours alone together and how they acted was their own concern. She had got to realize once and for all, she had no hold over Paul whatsoever.

She suggested she would like to go home, soon after it became evident that Paul and Ruth had left. Lewis seemed quite willing to take her and she said good night to Tony and collected her wrap.

They took a taxi back to the apartment as Lewis had

not brought his car this evening, and Karen wished that he had not wanted to accompany her inside. She did not feel in the mood for any more arguments.

However, Lewis said, as soon as they were inside the flat:

"Are you all right, Karen?"

"Am I all right?" she echoed in surprise. "Of course I am. Why?"

"Well, I seem to have spoilt your evening," he answered awkwardly. "Stoker probably thought me a complete idiot."

Karen flung her wrap over the couch and poured out two vodka and limes before replying. She handed a drink to Lewis and sipped her own.

"Well," she said brightly, "you were hardly the life and soul of the party, but don't let it upset you. You didn't really spoil my evening."

"Thank heavens for that. But you seem . . . remote . . . somehow."

Karen shrugged. "I'm probably just lost in thought," she remarked dryly. She looked at Lewis's slim shoulders and slender body. After seeing Paul, he seemed less of a man somehow. Lewis could never protect a woman by brute force should the need arise. Of course, in Lewis's uneventful life that contingency was hardly likely to arise. Still, it was nice to feel protected when you were with a man.

"Thoughts," said Lewis, frowning, "And what is occupying your thoughts?"

"They're not for exhibition," replied Karen, finishing her drink.

"Are you seeing Stoker again?"

Karen shook her head. "It was not that kind of association. I was just helping to fill in for his partner who let him down at the last minute. You look for attraction where there is none, Lewis."

Lewis's pale cheeks flushed. "I'm sorry," he said stiffly. "However, I must disagree with you. Stoker was positively drooling over you, whatever you might have thought."

"Oh, please," said Karen wearily. "Don't let's have an argument, Lewis. I'm not seeing Tony again. Of that you can be sure. Satisfied?"

"I suppose so." Lewis finished his drink too and replaced his glass on the tray.

"And now I must hurry you away," said Karen, abruptly. "I'm tired. Do you mind?"

"No. I'll go, Karen. We'll discuss this again at some more reasonable hour."

"There's nothing to discuss," retorted Karen, sighing. She held open the door. "Good night, Lewis."

Lewis left, leaving an atmosphere of brooding annoyance behind him, and something more. A menacing feeling of being caught in a spider's web. She had been intensely conscious that he had wanted to touch her, kiss her. She had prayed he would not do so and he had not. And yet the feeling remained. His attitude towards her showed a kind of obsession. From the very first she had been aware he was immensely drawn towards her. She had never encouraged him, but he had assumed over the years that she was happy with him, and might grow to love him. She knew now that this was impossible. Even without Paul's dominance of her being, Lewis just wasn't the kind of man she would choose for a husband. He was too possessive, too set in his ways, too old.

Closing the door after him, she heaved a sigh of relief. She sank down on to a couch and shivered uncontrollably. She felt sick and it was a mixture of fear and anti-climatic anticipation that had caused it.

Of one thing she was glad. She had seen Paul's fiancée tonight and now she knew her opposition. She was a very attractive woman, Karen had to admit, and had a neat, rounded figure. Restlessly, Karen rose and walked to the full-length mirror in her bedroom, twisting round before it and studying her own reflection. If Ruth was Paul's idea of perfection, it was little wonder that he had been willing to divorce Karen. Whereas Ruth's figure was delicately proportioned, Karen herself seemed tall and full-bodied; full breasts and curved thighs smoothed down to slender legs, and her hair was as straight as Ruth's was curly. They had absolutely nothing in common and Karen felt sure that if she spoke to her she would like her even less.

Ruth was the fragile lily, whereas Karen likened herself to a full-blooming rose. Which would stand the test of time? Karen hoped she would. At least her bone structure was good.

But then, perhaps Ruth made Paul feel strong and protective, appealing to his masculinity. Karen had always been too independent and she wondered whether Paul wanted a more submissive wife, one he could bend to his will. Still, whatever else, the sexual side of their marriage had always been perfect, and he could surely not improve on that.

Recalling their life together brought a lump to her throat. If Paul had not been so intent on making money, in improving an organization that was already powerful, they might have stood a chance.

But what woman wanted to spend her days and nights alone, week after week, while her husband served his other mistress, his other obsession, the company?

Even so, she knew that galling though it might seem, were he to command her now to come to him she would obey.

A week passed slowly. Karen was busy and buried herself in her work. It was a way of dismissing reality from her mind and she hoped her work wouldn't suffer in consequence. Tony Stoker rang up and thanked her for making his evening so pleasant. Karen was touched that he should be so thoughtful, particularly after Lewis's unveiled hostility. Lewis sent her a basket of spring flowers with a note apologizing for his ill-humour on the night of the ball, and Karen felt relieved. It seemed that the business with Lewis was not going to get out of hand after all.

About ten days after the ball, Karen found she had completed all the work she had in hand, and as it was all ready after lunch she decided against going in to the office. She could go in the following morning and see Lewis.

Feeling at quite a loose end, she decided to get her old Morris out of the garage and go for a drive. It was a long time since she had driven out of London, and the day was fresh and spring-like.

Donning her sheepskin coat over blue slacks and a blouse, she went down to the garages and rescued the car. She filled the tank with petrol at the nearest garage and drove out towards Guildford. The direction always intrigued her, for she had travelled this way many times with Paul.

The old car spun along merrily. She was very fond of it, and it had never let her down yet. She had bought it second-hand soon after leaving Paul, and it came in handy on occasions like this. She seldom used it to run around London, however, for the parking problem was too prevalent. Besides, there were always buses, and on special occasions, taxis.

She felt like a prisoner escaping for a while, and felt almost guilty about leaving London behind.

The hedges were all splitting now with their new greenery and the sides of the roads and the passing gardens were a riot of colour. It gave her a sense of well-being that she had not experienced for a long time.

She drove as far as Guildford, then made her way slowly back to London, but took the back roads through Old Woking and Chertsey. She found herself driving along the road off which branched the private road to Trevayne and her heart pounded sickeningly. Had her unconscious being brought her this way purposely?

She reached the turning and slowed the car. The roads were quiet and on a sudden impulse she turned into the private road. She only hesitated a moment before accelerating up the hill to the wrought-iron gates. She stopped the car and sat looking up the drive. The house looked exactly as it had done when she left it. She might never have been away. Smoke curled from one chimney and the white façade was immaculate as ever.

With a sigh she slid out of the car. She wondered who lived there now. Did they have any children? Was it a happy house? She hoped so. It had always been a wrench when she thought of Trevayne.

Curiosity overwhelmed her inhibitions, and she crossed the gateway and looked up the drive. Feeling like a conspirator she viewed the front of the building thoroughly. And then, quite suddenly, she saw the low white saloon that was parked to one side of the curved forecourt. It was exactly like Paul's car in which he had given her the lift.

Frowning, she drew out her cigarettes and lit one. Of course, it couldn't be Paul's car, for what would he be doing here? Unless, of course, the people who had bought the house were friends of his. Perhaps he was visiting them with Ruth.

She decided it would be safest to make a swift retreat before she was arrested for being a "peeping Tom". She turned suddenly, and in doing so caught her heel in a clump of turf.

Without any warning her ankle twisted painfully, and she was caught off balance and flung on to the gravel driveway. A sob stifled in her throat; she grasped her ankle tightly, willing the pain to go away. It was excruciating for a while and the tears came to her eyes.

As the worst of the jab receded she sat up awkwardly and rubbed the ankle briskly. She lifted her foot into its normal position. The ankle was very tender and even her fingers were rough with it.

She felt absolutely ridiculous sitting there and she prayed the pain would go away sufficiently to allow her to drive home. It was her right ankle and it was going to be awkward. Already the ankle was swelling and an angry redness disfigured the skin.

She was mentally chastising herself for being so careless and for coming here, nosing, in the first place. It was so embarrassing whoever owned the house, and if anyone should come out she would look pretty stupid. Heaven help her if Ruth was there. She would really get a laugh at Karen's expense. And if they were strangers they would want to know who she was and why she was snooping around in the first place.

And then, as though to punish her even more, the front door of the house was opened. Trembling a little, Karen did not wait to see who it was. She reached for the gatepost and tried unsuccessfully to stand up. However, her legs were so shaky and her foot so painful that she lost her balance and fell again to the gravel, the sharp stones grazing her fingers.

A man's voice came to her ears. He was saying:

"All right, Benson. I'll let you know next week ..." It was Paul's voice and it suddenly broke off as though he had just caught sight of her.

She did not dare to look, and closed her eyes in annoyance. Would he think she was following him or something? She heard the crunch of footsteps approaching her down the gravel drive. Then firm hands gripped her shoulders and she was helped to her feet and held firmly. She was turned to face him and she heard his sharp intake of breath.

"Karen!" he exclaimed, as he looked down at her. "What in God's name are you doing?"

Karen's face was pale, but she managed to say brightly:

"Squatting, darling. I'm afraid I've made rather a fool of myself."

Paul held her for a moment and she was glad. She dreaded his letting go for she might collapse, and then he would have to see her foot.

Paul frowned, obviously intrigued, and Karen decided

she would have to make the effort.

"I must apologize," she said, flushing. "I stopped to look at the house and I slipped over. I . . . I'll go now."

Turning on her good foot, she tried to limp to her car, but the foot refused to bear her weight and she fell, ignominiously, at his feet.

"Karen!" he exclaimed, sinking down on to his haunches beside her. "Are you ill? My God, look at your ankle!"

"It's nothing," she began, feeling stupid and weak, but he ignored her protest and slid his arms beneath her, picking her up easily in his arms.

For a moment they looked into each other's eyes and her heart raced madly. To be so close to him was at once exhilarating and overpowering.

He turned and strode back up the drive to the house, and carried her up the steps, across the terrace, and into the house, past the startled Benson who was wondering what was going on.

"Why, it's Mrs. Frazer!" he exclaimed, astonished.

Karen managed to smile, although actually she felt as though she was dreaming and that all this was not real.

"Hello, Benson," she said. "It's nice to see you again. Is Maggie well?"

"Very well," said Benson, still bewildered at this turn of events. "Is there anything you want, sir?"

"Yes," said Paul at once, halting in his tracks. "Ask Maggie to bring some cold water and an elastic bandage. I think Mrs. . . . I mean Miss Stacey . . . has sprained her ankle."

"Yes, sir," said Benson, and hurried off down the hall to the kitchen, after closing the front doors.

Paul carried Karen into the lounge and laid her on the settee. She looked about her in surprise. She remembered this room well. She had decided on the blue and grey décor, giving the room a restful air. The walls were a pale blue and two Impressionist paintings relieved their almost stark blankness. A carved mirror almost covered a third wall and french windows opened out of the fourth on to a tiled patio which had screens which could be slid back on warm summer days. The couch she was now lying on was of a deep blue brocade, and was large enough to seat four people.

The window hangings were of grey velvet, while the carpet was pearl grey Aubusson. White leather armchairs were set near the fireplace, which was concealed by a screen. There was no fire burning today.

From her seat on the couch Karen could see out of the french windows, and saw the stretch of lawn leading down to the swimming pool, drained now, and the tennis courts beyond.

She sighed and looked down at her swollen ankle. It was very awkward. The house was obviously just as she had left it and it intrigued her. Hadn't Paul told her he intended buying Ruth a house in the Sussex Weald?

She looked up at him. He was standing with his back to the fireplace.

"I'm sorry to be such a nuisance," she murmured, looking up at him.

"That's all right," he replied, his eyes dark and unfathomable. "Would you like a cigarette?"

"Thank you." She took one and Paul put one between his own lips. He lit them from his lighter and then slipped it back in his pocket as he straightened up.

"Tell me," said Karen, unable to restrain herself. "Do you still own this house?"

Paul drew on his cigarette, inhaling deeply and allowing the smoke to drift out slowly through his finely chiselled lips. His eyes returned to her.

"Yes." He looked at her gravely.

Karen shrugged and shook her head. "But you told me you were going to buy a house in Sussex!" she exclaimed. "Have you changed your mind?"

"No." Paul was enigmatic.

"Then why do you need this house?" she exclaimed in bewilderment.

"I don't *need* it," he replied coolly. "I simply don't want to sell it."

"I see. Curiouser and curiouser, as Alice said."

"You need not concern yourself," he said abruptly. "The house pleases me. It always did."

"Oh," she murmured. That quelled any ideas she might have had. Suddenly, her ankle twinged painfully, and she winced visibly, suppressing a cry.

Paul frowned, seeing this, and walked swiftly to the door.

"Hurry up, Maggie," he called impatiently.

"She's probably being as quick as she can," exclaimed Karen, turning round and looking at him, tall and handsome as he stood in the doorway.

"That's not quick enough," he retorted bluntly, but had hardly finished speaking before Mrs. Benson came hurrying across the hall towards him, complete with a dish of cold water and bandages.

"Where is Mrs. Frazer?" she exclaimed, brushing past Paul into the lounge.

"I'm here, Maggie," said Karen, smiling. "It's good to see you again."

"You should come to see us more often," exclaimed Maggie, tactlessly. "You know we'd like to hear how you're getting on."

Paul strolled back to them. "I'll do it, Maggie," he said, before she had time to get down on her knees. He took the dish. "Do you think you could rustle up some tea for us?"

"With pleasure," said Mrs. Benson, smiling benignly at Karen. "The kettle won't take a minute to boil. I'll not be long, sir."

Paul nodded, and Mrs. Benson departed, closing the lounge door behind her. Paul dropped his cigarette into the empty fire grate, and hitching up his trousers, knelt down beside the couch. He rolled back the trouser leg of her slacks to her shin and had a good look at the reddened skin.

With cool, exploring fingers, he examined the ankle. "There are no bones broken," he said quietly.

"Oh – good," she managed to say, only conscious of the gentle touch of his fingers. It was a delight to feel his hands touching her again, and the subsequent pain as he bound up the ankle was of secondary importance. He soaked the bandage well before applying it to her ankle and he bound it firmly but not tightly. The coolness was very welcome, and when he had completed his task, he secured it with a safety-pin. Karen waited with clenched fists for him to pull down her trouser leg over the bandage, willing herself to remain calm. The moments of delight were over, and she must not betray her feelings.

But suddenly his fingers gripped her foot tightly, and she looked down to find that he was making no effort to rise from his position. Instead, he was caressing her foot with a strange intensity and when he looked up and met her startled gaze his eyes darkened passionately.

Karen's limbs turned to water at that look, and she shook her head incredulously as his hands slid up her body to her shoulders, and he stretched his length beside her, seeking her mouth with his own.

"Paul!" she breathed hesitantly, turning her head away, but one hand gripped her throat and he turned her mouth to meet his. Her lips parted involuntarily and his kiss seemed to draw the very strength out of her body. It was a very satisfying kiss, hardening and lengthening, until Karen felt herself sliding down into an oblivion of feeling where nothing mattered but that Paul should go on making love to her. He was not gentle, only demanding, and she responded with equal fervour.

They had both forgotten the imminent arrival of Mrs. Benson and only the sound of the tea trolley being wheeled across the hall brought them back to reality.

With a sound that was almost a groan, Paul dragged himself up from the couch, away from her, his fingers not quite steady as he straightened his tie and ran a hasty hand over his thick black hair.

Karen sat up again on the couch. Her face was flushed from his kisses and her hair was in wild disorder after being pressed against the cushions. With the prosaic admittance of Mrs. Benson, she tried rather unsuccessfully to smooth her silky hair, but it clung against her cheeks. She wondered what Mrs. Benson could be thinking as she put the trolley beside the couch so that Karen could pour the tea. She must be aware that something had been going on and Karen knew she was infinitely curious. But, like the well-trained servant she was, she merely said:

"Will you pour, madam?"

"Yes, thank you," said Karen, smiling self-consciously at her. "It looks very nice." On the trolley was a teapot, milk jug, sugar basin, cups and saucers, and a plate of freshly baked, buttered scones.

"Very well, madam. Ring if you need any more tea."

Mrs. Benson withdrew after scarcely glancing at Paul, who was helping himself to a drink from the cocktail cabinet.

Karen poured the tea, feeling very strange. Now that it was over, she felt ashamed and annoyed with herself for responding so completely to him. He would probably think she was the epitome of everything he most abhorred, for although he had kissed her, she felt sure he was hating himself for doing so.

Forcing herself to be natural, she said: "Do you want any tea?"

Paul swung round, a glass in his hand. "No, thanks," he muttered, in a low voice.

Karen shrugged and sipped her own. The tea was relaxing but the thought of food nauseated her. She finished the tea and replaced the cup on the trolley. Paul lit a cigarette and then he said:

"I must apologize," in a tight voice. He ran a finger round the inside of his collar. "I'm afraid . . . I made a fool of myself."

Karen's cheeks burned. "Don't perturb yourself," she

said quietly. "It was a mutual reaction to a set of circumstances."

Paul took a mouthful of his whisky, and drew on his cigarette.

"I'm . . . er . . . I'm glad you realize that was all it was," he said awkwardly. "I was afraid you might for a moment think . . ."

Karen interrupted him. "Don't go on, Paul. It's quite all right. I know how you feel."

"Damn you, do you?" he muttered angrily. His eyes narrowed disbelievingly. "I really don't believe that you do, Karen. Don't you secretly cherish the thought that I still really love you and that I'm simply burying my sorrows with Ruth?"

Karen's eyes widened. What had brought this on?

"Paul!" she exclaimed reproachfully.

Paul bit his lip angrily. "Oh, Karen, don't play the innocent with me. It just isn't you! You have always believed you could act as you like, treat people as you like. Well, in my case, it's simply not coming off. I'm marrying Ruth because I want to, not to forget you. And any part of me that reacts to you is inspired by a purely sexual reaction. Do you understand? You're a very beautiful woman. I've always thought so."

Karen felt suddenly furiously angry. How dare he speak to her like that. She felt she was about six inches high and that he was stooping to even speak to her. He wasn't even near the truth. Of course, she had sometimes prayed he still loved her, but as of this moment she felt sure she had been imagining a lot of things. She felt the pain in her ankle and wished she could get up this minute and run out of here, away from him and his hateful comments. But she could not. She was tied to the couch for the time being and was forced to endure whatever else was to come.

She bent her head, and looked intently at her fingernails to avoid looking at him. The only saving in his remarks had been when he said she was physically attractive to him. Wanting to hurt him now as he had hurt her, she swung her legs to the ground and said:

"And is your dear fiancée aware of your ... er ... sexual reaction to me? I mean ... have you discussed it over lunch or something?"

She was maliciously glad when she saw him look uncomfortable and turn away, drawing on his cigarette. She had certainly chosen the right reply to his comments. Although she felt she was acting by remote control, Karen now felt in a more favourable situation. Now she had him on the mental hook.

"Don't be coarse," he snapped angrily.

Karen managed a half laugh. "Darling," she exclaimed, "where's your sense of humour? Oh, I can quite see that telling Ruth wouldn't be very practical, would it?"

"Shut up!" he muttered, swinging round on her.

"Why? I'm only telling the truth, Paul. I'm sure Ruth wouldn't find it at all understandable; your being interested in me, I mean. Nor should I in her position. She might think you were still hankering after old times."

"You killed any love I had for you two years ago," he said, his face grim. "In a divorce court, or had you forgotten? There, is that blatant enough for you? O.K., you want it out in the open, now you've got it."

"You divorced me, remember?" she said, through tight lips.

"Do I?" he groaned, clenching his fists.

He stubbed out his cigarette in a brass ashtray and paced up and down. Then after a while he turned on her again.

"Do you honestly believe that I might consider taking you back after you've been Martin's mistress?"

Karen's face burned. She put up her hands and covered her cheeks. God, what did he think of her?

"I was never Martin's mistress," she spat angrily. "Not

then, or now. That was a gorgeous story you concocted to give me my freedom, as you put it at the time. Or was it you who wanted to be free? Then of course, Lewis's visits to the apartment made very interesting evidence..."

"Very interesting," agreed Paul coldly. "I suppose you say they were innocent?"

"Yes, I do. Good heavens, Paul, do you think I could become seriously involved with a man more than twenty years my senior? Besides, Lewis is not my type."

"Do you seriously expect me to believe that?" he exclaimed sceptically.

"Please yourself," replied Karen, feeling chilled to the bone.

Paul crossed to the window. "And are you going to tell Ruth how I... well... feel?" he asked slowly.

Karen gasped. "Hell, what an opinion you have of me!" she cried in exasperation. "I have no intention of blackmailing you if that's what you mean. You simply amuse me, that's all."

"Do I?" he muttered angrily, swinging round, his eyes glittering. He took a step towards her and Karen's body froze into immobility.

But whatever he was about to say or do was interrupted by a light knock on the door.

Paul thrust his hands into his trousers pockets. "Come in," he muttered, and Benson put his head round the door.

"Sorry to intrude, sir," he began, "but will you be staying for dinner, after all?"

Paul looked thoughtfully at Karen and hesitated for only a moment.

"No," he replied abruptly. "We'll be leaving almost immediately. Will you put Miss Stacey's car in the garage for tonight, and I'll have Edwards collect it tomorrow. He can take it back to town. Miss Stacey is not in a fit state to drive tonight. I'll take her back to town myself."

"Very good, sir," said Benson promptly, but Karen protested.

"It's not necessary that you should take me," she exclaimed. But Paul silenced her by a pointed glance at her foot and she had to give in. It was true, her foot would not have the strength to work the pedals in the car. She was virtually at his mercy and she cursed her ankle anew. Because of it so many things had happened and so much had been said.

And yet, she thought wryly, she would not have wanted to relinquish those moments when Paul was making love to her. She would treasure those.

"Right," said Paul, dismissing Benson. "I expect to see you later in the week."

Benson smiled at Karen. "Will your ankle be all right, madam?"

"I think so, thanks," said Karen, smiling in return. "It's been so nice seeing you, Benson."

"It's been nice to see you, too, madam," replied Benson warmly, and with a nod to Paul he left them.

Karen gripped the side of the couch and tried to stand up. She managed to balance on one leg, stork-like, but Paul moved forward and before she had a chance to protest, lifted her into his arms. He was not prepared to let her stagger out to the car.

His face was so close, only an enormous effort of willpower prevented her from touching him.

He carried her out to the car and put her into the front beside the driver's seat. Then he walked round the bonnet and slid in beside her.

Mr. and Mrs. Benson came to the door to wave and they watched the car purr away down the drive. The powerful engine opened up as they descended the hill, and then they were out on the open road again.

Karen shivered. "I adore this car," she said, without being able to prevent herself.

"Good!" He raised his eyebrows and looked quizzically at her. "You'll be happy to learn that I chose it myself.

It's a Facel Vega."

Karen was impressed in spite of herseif. "You never drove anything like this in the old days."

Paul couldn't suppress an amused exclamation. "You preferred the Rolls, as I recall," he remarked dryly. "I simply felt like a change."

"Well, it's certainly luxurious," she said lightly.

Paul drove expertly and Karen thoroughly enjoyed the feeling of being with him again. The incident at the house was pushed into the back of her mind, and she determined to keep their conversation in this light vein.

As they neared her apartment, Paul said: "Give me your garage key, Karen, and I'll have Edwards put the car away when he brings it up tomorrow. He can leave the keys with the hall porter and you can collect them from him."

"All right," Karen rummaged through her purse, looking for the garage keys. After searching for several minutes, during which time the car halted outside the block of apartments, she still could not find the keys. "I must have left them all in the car," she said apologetically. "I have a spare key in the apartment, and that will be better because there are quite a lot of keys on the key-ring in the car, and it would take him some time to distinguish one from the other. If you care to come up to the apartment I could give you the one key necessary."

Paul looked strangely and intently at her, and with an exclamation of annoyance she emptied the contents of her purse on to the seat between them. There were some scribbled notes for shopping, her wallet-purse, a lipstick and powder compact and a pair of ear-rings. There were no keys.

"Satisfied?" she asked angrily, staring at him. "If you wait here I'll go and get the blasted key and bring it down to you. You're obviously terrified to come up."

"Terrified?" he muttered, softly and menacingly.

"Yes, terrified," she replied bravely. "Don't alarm yourself. I won't try to vamp you."

Paul half smiled, and slid out of the car. Before he had circled the bonnet, Karen had slid out also and hopped on one leg up the steps to the entrance hall. It was a slow and awkward business, but she was determined to be independent.

Shrugging his broad shoulders, he followed her. She said a few words to the hall porter and was on her way again before he caught up with her. Then he said:

"Tired?"

"No, I can manage. Don't you dare touch me."

Paul shook his head and followed her into the lift.

It was nearly six-thirty when Karen reached the apartment. She had borrowed the pass key from the porter to open her apartment as all her keys were still on the key-ring at Trevayne.

Inside, the apartment was warm and attractive, and Karen hopped inside awkwardly, allowing him to follow her if he chose. She half expected him to wait on the doorstep, but he followed her in and closed the door firmly, leaning back against it. It was his first real chance to see the place in which she was living and he looked round with undisguised interest.

Karen removed her sheepskin coat and crossed the lounge slowly to the bedroom. Her spare keys were in the dressing-table drawer, and she retrieved them and came back into the lounge to find Paul wandering around, studying the paintings on the walls.

Karen hesitated. "Dare I offer you a drink?" she asked pointedly.

Paul swung round and smiled. "I guess so," he answered smoothly. "But don't disturb yourself, I'll get it."

He poured two whiskies, adding some soda to one and handed it to her. Then he resumed his wanderings. The abstract paintings obviously interested him, for he was studying each one in turn.

He turned round as she dropped down on to the couch. "These are exceptionally good," he said, nodding to the pictures. "Who did them?"

"Me," she replied at once, rather ungrammatically.

"You!" he echoed. "Really? I never knew you were interested in this kind of art. I thought your designing was all that interested you."

Karen shrugged her slim shoulders. "It's my hobby. I have a lot of spare time and I've taken up the other end of the artist's brush."

Paul nodded slowly. "You never cease to amaze me," he remarked dryly. "But tell me, you must know they're good. Have you tried to sell them?"

Karen shook her head. "Let's be realistic, Paul," she said. "There are dozens of artists trying to sell this kind of thing. It's in vogue now. What chance would I have? Besides, Lewis thinks . . ." She broke off, annoyed with herself for bringing Lewis's name into it.

Paul's eyes narrowed. "Yes? And what does Martin think?"

Karen bit her lip. "Well . . . he thinks they're all right, but definitely non-commercial. Rather amusing for my entertainment, but dull."

Paul raised his eyebrows and looked very surprised. He swallowed the rest of his drink.

"Does he now?" he said thoughtfully. "Then I'm afraid that not for the first time, I must disagree with him. I think they're very good. So much so that I should like to buy one myself."

Karen's face was scarlet. "Oh, please, Paul," she cried, "don't mention money between us." She got up and turned away. "If there's one you would like, I'll willingly give it to you. Goodness knows, I have plenty."

Paul's eyes narrowed. "That's hardly businesslike," he remarked dryly.

Karen swung round on her good foot. "Do we have to be businesslike with each other?"

Paul shrugged and poured himself a second drink.

"All right," he said easily. He crossed the room to a bright, vivid painting splashed with reds and greens and yellows. "I'd like this one," he said thoughtfully. "It reminds me of the sunsets we used to see from the windows at Trevayne."

"How clever of you," she said, smiling. "That's exactly what it is intended to be."

He looked at her intently. "Yes. Well, we always had an affinity in things, remember?"

Karen shivered. Did she remember? If he only knew how tortuous those memories still were.

"I remember," she murmured softly, and he swallowed the remainder of his drink.

"I must go," he said, a trifle thickly. "I have an appointment."

"All right, Paul." She lifted down the picture. "You might as well take it with you."

He took it from her, carefully avoiding any contact with her skin.

"Who knows?" he remarked dryly. "It may be worth a fortune, one day."

"I should say that was hardly likely," replied Karen quietly. "Oh, here's the garage key, and would you give the pass key back to the porter, please?"

He fingered the keys. "All right," he murmured. "Look after your ankle, won't you?"

"Do you really care, Paul?" she asked mockingly, trying to disperse the air of melancholy she was feeling at his departure. The last few minutes had been so deliciously natural and now he was going back to Ruth.

"Yes, I care," he muttered, and turning, he walked out of the apartment, banging the door behind him.

Karen stared after him, her heart thumping. Just what had that remark implied? Nothing like so much as she imagined, she was sure, but it was nice to think that they had parted on better terms.

She hobbled over to the wall where the painting had hung. Not for anything would she have told him that that was her own favourite. It was sufficient to know that he had it and might look at it sometimes. Would he think of her when he did so? She hoped so. At least a small part of his attention would be hers sometimes and the idea was warming.

She sighed and lit a cigarette. In a little over two months he would be married again. Two months! Could she bear the idea? And when it was all over she would continually think of them together and envy Ruth. Was life going to be worth living? She felt the now ever-ready tears pricking at her eyes. Might it not be as well for her to leave England all together? She could probably get a job in South Africa or Australia if she really wanted to. She had good qualifications and Lewis could vouch for her. If he would? It might be just what she needed. A change of air.

But then the thought of being thousands of miles away from Paul did not much agree with her. At least here in London he could contact her if he ever needed her. In Australia he would not know where to find her. She could hardly give him a forwarding address. No. She would stay. At least for the time being. There were still two months before the fatal event.

CHAPTER FIVE

About a week later, Paul was about to leave his office to go out to lunch when the internal telephone pealed. Frowning, he lifted the receiver, and to his surprise Simon's voice answered him:

"Paul, I'm glad I've caught you. Could I see you right away?"

Paul glanced at his watch. He had an engagement for lunch with a textile merchant from the Midlands. They were to have lunch at the Bermudan, which was a large hotel near the office building, and as the appointment was not until one o'clock, he had twenty minutes to spare.

"All right, Simon," he said, a little impatiently. What on earth could Simon want now? "Will you come up here?"

"Yes, I'll come right up." Simon rang off, and Paul lay back in his chair, thoughtfully studying the telephone. He hoped Simon was not in more trouble.

Remembering the business of Simon and Sandra brought back memories of Karen and their last meeting together. His thoughts had turned often in that direction since he had seen her, and he wondered what she had thought of him. He pondered too, on what might have happened had he kissed her in that way at her apartment instead of at Trevayne. At the apartment they would have been completely alone and undisturbed without Mrs. Benson to interrupt them with a tea trolley. It was quite a thought, and he felt the blood heat in his veins at the memory of her warm mouth. It was all right telling yourself coldly and logically that you had no intention of becoming emotionally involved with any woman, ever again, but when the practical aspects of such a theory were put to the test, the solution was not so simple. And he was convinced that Ruth would never disturb his deeper emotions whatever situation they were presented with. That, too, was quite a thought.

When Simon arrived, Paul's secretary showed him in. He looked rather anxious and agitated and stood before Paul's desk, fidgeting with his tie.

"Well, Simon," said Paul, swinging his chair backwards and forwards in a circular movement as was the usual motion of these chairs. His cool eyes surveyed his brother's flushed face. "Is something wrong?"

"Yes, that is ..." Simon sank down into the chair opposite him. "Paul, I'm not finding this easy, and you're not making it any easier."

"I'm sorry about that," remarked Paul, rather dryly. "Come on, Simon. I've a luncheon appointment at one. Get it over with. Is it money?"

"No. It's Sandra Stacey." It came out with a rush.

Paul stopped swinging his chair abruptly. "What?"

"You heard," said Simon awkwardly. "I've been meeting her. Since we had our little ... chat."

"I see." Paul sounded uncompromising.

"Have you nothing to say?" Simon asked, desperately.

"I'm saving judgment," replied Paul slowly. "I'm giving you credit in that I believe there must be an explanation for this. Is there?"

"Yes – that is, you might not think it sufficient."

"Well, do go on," muttered Paul, trying to contain his annoyance.

"Sandra started telephoning me, after I stopped seeing her. She even went so far as to ring me at home. She also wrote me letters, you can imagine the kind of letters, I suppose and ... well ... Julia started getting angry and I agreed to meet Sandra to call it off."

Paul helped himself to a cigarette from the box on his desk and flicked his lighter. He replaced the lighter in his pocket and continued his study of his brother.

"Well," continued Simon, "when we met she started

threatening all sorts of things if I called it off. I was stupid, I know, but I allowed her to win. Anyway, now, things are getting out of hand. She's wanting more than I'm prepared to give her ... marriage, for one thing."

"I really can't understand your mentality," said Paul, shaking his head, "Good God, man, what did you see in her in the first place? She's not your usual type of girlfriend. She dresses abominably."

"That's only your opinion," retorted Simon heatedly. "She's really a sweet kid."

"Then marry her," drawled Paul coolly.

Simon moved restlessly, fingering his tie, "Julia ... she would never divorce me," he said lamely.

"She would if I made a generous settlement on her," replied Paul calmly. "Haven't you noticed? It's money that interests Julia. You're her meal ticket at the moment, but if she was rich enough to supply her own, who knows what she might do?"

"All right," muttered Simon. "You've made your point."

"I have indeed. You don't want a divorce from Julia. You like your comfortable, no strings attached, relationship. Be honest with yourself and admit it."

"All right," said Simon. "All right, I agree. So help me."

"Why should I help you?" asked Paul grimly. "I ought to let you stew in your own juice. If it was any other girl but Sandra Stacey I would do so."

"I know. But you'll do something because she's Karen's sister,"

"Because she's a seventeen-year-old without any sense," corrected Paul, angry himself now. He did not intend discussing Karen with his brother.

"Have it your way," said Simon, shrugging. "I just want to be free of entanglements. Understand?"

"Perfectly. So, from now on, no matter what Sandra says you will not meet her. I'll arrange for you to leave

London for a while and when you get back I may have resolved the problem once and for all."

"Good. But try and keep that little ... so-and-so away from me."

"I can't imagine what she sees in a spineless creature like you," said Paul, sighing.

"It's the Frazer charm," said Simon laconically. "Or don't you use yours, brother dear?"

Paul's eyes were icy. "Get out of here," he snapped menacingly, "before I really lose my temper."

"I'm going, thanks for your time." Simon sounded sarcastic as he slammed the door behind him.

Paul sighed heavily. He would be glad when Simon became able to handle his life more intelligently.

He stared moodily into space. He had to admit that this time Simon was not entirely to blame. Sandra was definitely at fault. A man could only become close to a woman if the woman was agreeable. It was logical that given the chance, any man would take advantage of it. Was that what had happened in their case? Had Sandra flung herself at his head from the beginning? But how far had it gone? He prayed Sandra had not gone too far. Was she that foolish? Perhaps she really thought she loved him. Many women seemed to find him attractive. To a teenager, used to pallid youths, Simon might have seemed love's young dream.

He frowned and drew on his cigarette. But that did not alter anything. Simon was married, and married men were not to be played with. Not even by their contemporaries, let alone adolescents.

Still in a disturbed frame of mind he met Arnold Gibson for lunch. Throughout the meal he remained taciturn and introspective, which was quite unlike his usual self. In consequence, very little of importance was discussed or decided upon and a further meeting had to be arranged. Paul felt he would not have been surprised if Gibson had decided to go elsewhere to execute his business. He had been rude and non-committal and

Gibson was quite within his rights to object and expect better from him.

But fortunately, Gibson was an understanding man and he quite realized that something was troubling his companion. They parted on the best of terms with an arrangement to meet another day.

Paul was therefore in a savage frame of mind when he went back to his office at about three o'clock. He secretary, who was quite used to his moods, was surprised at his apparent animosity, and Paul had to apologize to her after snapping unreasonably at her.

"Forgive me," he murmured, a half apologetic smile on his face. "I'm sorry to be such a bear."

Miss Hopper smiled. "That's all right, Mr. Frazer. I know you had Mr. Simon in here earlier on."

Paul smiled in return. He could understand now how she had understood in the first place. The whole office building was aware of Simon's indiscretions. He never made any attempt to keep his affairs private.

After Miss Hopper had gone he lit a cigarette. He had got to find a solution to Sandra Stacey's problem. It was typically Simon to get himself into a mess and expect someone else to get him out of it.

A solution began forming in his mind as the afternoon wore on and as it did so his mood improved. If he could get this off his back he would feel entirely relaxed instead of wondering and dreading what might happen next.

Leaning forward abruptly, he lifted the receiver of his personal private outside line. He dialled the number of Karen's apartment with a strange feeling, almost like reluctance. He had got to speak to her, however, so he might as well get it over with. The telephone rang at the other end of the line.

After what seemed like an age, when Paul was considering replacing the receiver and ringing later, the telephone was lifted, and Karen's rather breathless tones answered.

"Hello! Who is that?"

Paul hesitated only a moment. Then he said, rather roughly:

"Karen. It's me, Paul."

Karen felt her heart skip a beat when she heard the husky voice addressing her. Why was he calling her today? Surely it couldn't be about Sandra this time.

"Hello, Paul," she replied, trying to sound casual and composed. "Sorry to keep you waiting, but I was in the bath."

"Were you now?" He sounded amused. "Well, I'm sorry to have interrupted your ablutions, Karen, but our plans don't appear to have worked."

For a moment her mind went blank. "Plans?" she queried faintly.

"Sandra – and Simon," he explained impatiently. "Surely you haven't been sleeping in the bath?"

"No. At least, I don't think so." She chuckled a little. "I'm sorry, Paul."

Paul sighed. "Well, just be sure that you don't do anything so stupid," he adjured her harshly.

"Darling, do get on," she exclaimed, interrupting him. "I'm freezing, standing here in the altogether!"

"Karen!" he muttered reproachfully, and then he heaved a sigh. "Shall I ring back in a few minutes?"

"You could come round," she commented thoughtfully. "I'd endeavour to be dressed by then, of course."

"No, thanks." Paul was adamant. He was aware that if he succumbed to the temptations to do just that, goodness knew what might happen. She was deliberately arousing him, and the picture of her in the bath brought back memories he wanted to forget completely.

"All right, darling, fire away. I'll freeze a few moments longer. What has happened to Simon and Sandra?"

"They are still meeting."

"What?" Karen was astonished.

"Yes, I know they were until today anyway. I think

I've talked some sense into Simon now. We had quite a session this afternoon. Do you think you or your mother could do the same for Sandra? Apparently she has been running after him, ringing him up both here and at home, and writing him letters. That sort of thing."

"Oh, lord," Karen groaned. "Will she ever see sense, do you think?"

"I couldn't say. She's your sister. You know her better than I do. She really is the limit, though. And positively crazy about Simon. Simon came to see me today. That's how I found out."

Karen sounded annoyed. "I just can't think of anything to say to her, and you know what Mother is like."

"I know. Look, couldn't your mother and Sandra take a holiday abroad somewhere, away from London at any rate? A few weeks will give Simon time to find someone else. Besides, Sandra herself might find a new interest. She's young, and full of life, apparently. Although it seems that boys of her own age bore her. Why else could she be interested in Simon? He's a forbidden thrill."

"Like me," taunted Karen teasingly, and heard his sharp intake of breath. "But honestly, Paul, my mother isn't very well off. I don't suppose she could afford a holiday anywhere at the moment."

"I'm quite willing to finance the idea," remarked Paul coolly.

"No. No," cried Karen angrily. "Don't say such a thing, Paul. It has nothing to do with you."

"Oh, but it has. I want Simon to give Sandra up just as much as you do. She's far too young for him. If anything went seriously wrong, he would really be in a flat spin then."

"Well, I don't know what to say. It sounds now as though as I was assessing for the money."

"My dear Karen, I can afford it."

"I know, but ..." Her voice trailed away. "Anyway, you had better ring Mother and tell her. She would probably jump at the idea. She has no pride where money is concerned."

"Hurrah for her," said Paul, sounding amused. "Really, Karen, don't be so stand-offish and independent. I'd like to help you . . . all of you."

"But this is our problem," she exclaimed as a last attempt.

"You made it mine, too, remember," he said softly.

"Very well, have it your own way," she replied defeatedly.

Paul sounded irritated. "Look, Karen, I tell you what I will do. I'll pick you up at your apartment at about eight o'clock this evening and we will both go round and see Madeleine and Sandra. Right?"

Karen sighed, feeling her resistance sapping. To turn over the problem to Paul was such a wonderful thing to do. It was like having a fairy godfather. She had to capitulate.

"It sounds a great idea," she admitted quietly. "But won't . . . Ruth . . . object?"

"Why should she?" asked Paul abruptly. "Stop bringing my personal affairs into this. It only concerns your mother and Sandra. No one else."

"All right, honey," she exclaimed. "Don't snap my head off. But won't she expect to see you tonight?"

"Hardly," he replied sardonically. "She flew to the States a couple of days ago to bring over her parents for the wedding."

"Oh." Karen felt the familiar pain in her stomach. "All right, Paul, will you come up, or shall I come down to meet you?"

"I'll come up," he answered, sounding amused again. "Unless the lift gets stuck half-way, of course."

Karen chuckled and replaced her receiver. Although the affair of Sandra and Simon was a problem, she felt she ought to feel grateful to them for enabling her to meet Paul again.

And yet wasn't she just creating trouble for herself this

way? Paul might find it all an amusing episode and nothing more, while she was getting more emotionally involved every minute.

She heard the knock at the door at seven-thirty. She glanced at her watch in some surprise; he was early! She had been sitting on the couch, reading a magazine, and now she threw the magazine down and went to the door eagerly. She was wearing a shift of apricot jersey that combined deliciously with her creamy complexion and her hair was loose about her shoulders.

Flinging open the door, smiling welcomingly, she stepped back in obvious surprise and dismay when she found Lewis Martin outside.

"Why, Lewis!" she exclaimed. "This is a surprise!"

"Hello, Karen," he smiled. His keen eyes took in the apricot dress and her flushed cheeks and they narrowed a little. "You look very attractive," he went on. "I assume you're ready to go out."

"Yes, in a little while," she agreed awkwardly. "Would you like to come in?"

"Thank you." He stepped inside and with some reluctance Karen closed the door.

"Will you have a drink?" she asked, twisting her fingers together.

"Thank you again. A vodka, please."

Karen poured the drink and handed it to him. "Now," she said, trying to sound unconcerned, "what can I do for you?"

Lewis smiled. "I've called to see whether you're interested in taking on the new design for that special satin fabric which they're going to launch in August," he replied smoothly. "As I expected you to come into the office this week and you've disappointed me, I decided I would come round to see if you were all right. I see you are."

Karen felt on edge. Lewis had said nothing wrong and yet there was something menacing about his manner. It was odd, but recently she had felt this atmosphere around him. She could not define it, and eventually put it down to her own disturbed condition.

"Yes – well – may I let you know?" she said, flushing. "I'm still working on the carpets."

"Of course, my dear. No hurry." Then why have you come round here? she wanted to shout. Spying on me?

"Good!" Karen poured herself a sherry and sipped it earnestly. She wondered how long he intended to stay. If Paul had arrived to find Lewis here he would suspect the worst in the circumstances. Why, oh, why had Lewis chosen tonight to call?

She accepted a cigarette from him and glanced surreptitiously at her watch. Ten minutes to eight already.

Lewis did not sit down. He wandered round the room as Paul had done, looking at her paintings. Would he notice one was missing?

"I really can't understand why you waste so much of your energies on these," he said, deliberately, Karen thought.

"Can't you?" she asked, longing to make a retort about Paul's comments.

"No. You're so good at your work as a commercial designer, you ought to design originals for competition work."

"I prefer relaxation when I'm not working for you," she replied stiffly.

"Ah, yes." He swung round. "Relaxation is a great thing. And what would you say relaxed you?"

Karen frowned. What was he getting at now?

"Oh, painting ... and reading ... and driving ..." she said slowly.

"Driving! Yes, indeed. A very pleasant pastime," he murmured softly. "I saw an interesting car near here the other day."

"Did you?" Karen was frankly bored now. And Paul would be here at any moment.

"Yes, indeed. A Facel Vega, a cream Facel Vega."

Karen's tongue, which was moistening her lips, stopped in mid-air. Deciding to take the bull by the horns, she said defiantly:

"I believe Paul drives a cream Facel Vega."

Lewis did not look surprised, although he said: "Does he? I didn't know."

Karen was convinced that he did not know very well, and that this was his way of telling her he knew Paul had been to the flat. What was he thinking of? Was he having her followed? Or was he following her himself? She shivered involuntarily.

"He was here a few days ago," she said clearly. "He came to see my awful paintings. He thought they were good."

"Did he? How very interesting." Lewis's eyes narrowed coldly.

Suddenly there was another knock at the door. Ignoring Lewis, Karen thankfully went to answer it. It could only be Paul.

He stood on the threshold, dressed tonight in a dark blue suit and a thick camel-hair overcoat. He looked so handsome and familiar that Karen wanted to fling herself into his arms and risk the rebuffs which would surely come. He smiled at Karen and then saw Lewis. He glanced swiftly at Karen, but Karen was not going to have him walk out on her now. Sliding an arm through his, she drew him inside, saying:

"Lewis is just going, Paul." It was forcing Lewis's hand, but he merely nodded and replaced his glass on the tray. "I'll let you know about those designs in a day or so," she said, as he reached the door.

"Very well." Lewis inclined his head at Paul. "Good evening, Frazer."

Paul merely nodded his head but did not speak.

Karen closed the door thankfully after he had gone and leaned back against it. Then she straightened and looked across at Paul.

"For your information, he arrived at precisely seven-thirty," she stated clearly, a flush staining her creamy cheeks.

"You don't have to justify yourself to me," he replied, loosening his coat. "I like this apartment, Karen."

Karen sighed. "Would you like a drink?" she asked.

Paul smiled. "Thank you, yes. I'll get it." He crossed to the drinks and poured himself a whisky, but Karen did not want any more. Then he offered her a cigarette and lounged on to the couch. He looked very much at ease, almost at home, thought Karen, her spirits rising a little.

She drew on her cigarette and crossed the room restlessly.

"Sit down!" commanded Paul suddenly, and with an exclamation she subsided on to a low armchair.

"Now," he said quietly, "relax. I've not come here to quarrel with you, even if I did find Martin already in possession."

"Lewis possesses nothing; not me, at least," retorted Karen, sighing again. "Why do you have to say things like that, Paul?"

She rose abruptly to her feet and crossed the room again, but as she passed Paul he leaned forward and with tiger-like speed his fingers fastened round her wrist in a vice-like grip.

"What would you have me say?" he asked, his eyes brooding and intense.

"You're hurting me," she protested, trying to free her wrist.

"Am I?" He did not slacken his grip, but rose to his feet, his broad body towering over her. His nearness was almost too much for her. She had the strongest impulse to press herself against him. "Go on," he continued. "What would you like me to say? That I like your dress? That you look very beautiful tonight?"

Karen flushed. "No. I wouldn't presume to think such a thing," she replied. "Nothing as blatant as that. I know you're an engaged man too, you know. I just wish you wouldn't make veiled insinuations."

Paul's eyes darkened. "That man strips you naked every time he looks at you," he muttered violently. "If you can't see the look in his eyes, you must be incredibly naïve."

Karen wrenched herself away from him.

"You're crazy!" she exclaimed. "Lewis isn't like that." But even as she spoke the words she wondered if they were strictly true. Lewis had been more persistent of late.

"I think we'd better go," she said, reaching for her cream mohair coat. It was a beautiful coat that Paul had bought for her, and it enhanced the fairness of her complexion. If Paul recognized the coat he gave no sign and merely shrugged his assent at her suggestion.

The Facel Vega was parked below. It looked out of place in the rather subdued mews, but Karen felt the warmth flooding her body again when she realized she had an evening in Paul's company ahead of her.

Paul put her into the car and then walked lazily round the bonnet and slid in beside her behind the wheel. As they drove away, they passed a car parked in the dark pool at the far side of the mews. It was a dark saloon, and Karen had the strangest feeling that it was Lewis's car. Had he been watching to see how long Paul stayed in the apartment? The idea appalled and infuriated her. She wondered if she ought to mention her suspicions to Paul and then decided against it. He would be all for turning back and confronting him, and she felt she couldn't face another scene tonight.

But why was he there? Of what possible interest could their casual relationship be to him? Unless he was jealous. She remembered again his attitude the night of the ball. It was very worrying.

Paul glanced curiously at her a number of times as they drove the short distance to her mother's home. She had withdrawn into herself somehow, and he wished he knew what she was thinking.

They parked outside the house, and Karen slid out before he could come round to help her. Paul slid out also and they both reached the front door together. She inserted her key in the lock and they went inside. Paul was just behind her and the poignancy of the situation washed over her. The last time they had come here together they had still been married.

Liza, hearing them, appeared from the kitchen at once. She looked absolutely astounded to see Paul, and her astonishment showed in her open face.

"Why, Mr. Frazer, sir!" she cried. "What a shock you gave me!"

"I'm sorry, Liza," said Paul, smiling his attractive smile, and causing Liza to blush prettily and smooth down her apron in an attempt to appear unflustered.

"And how is my favourite housekeeper?" he asked, easily, loosening his overcoat.

Liza giggled merrily and Karen sighed. Paul could charm anyone, and Liza had always been an easy victim.

"Mrs. Stacey and Sandra are in the lounge," she said, indicating the closed door. "I believe they're watching television."

"Thank you, Liza," said Karen, glancing at Paul for a second. Then she moved forward and opened the lounge door.

As Liza had said, Madeline and her younger daughter were watching television, although Madeline was knitting as well, a vivid scarlet piece of work. Sandra was draped untidily in her chair, dressed in tight-fitting jeans and a skin-tight sweater with no sleeves. She looked bored and resentful, and when she saw Karen and Paul she sprang to her feet.

"Well, well," she exclaimed dramatically. "Look who's here! What are these, Mother? Reinforcements?"

Madeline thrust away her knitting and she too stood up, staring disbelievingly at Paul.

"Dear boy!" she cried. "What a wonderful surprise!"

Karen felt like saying that Paul was certainly no boy, but Madeline continued: "What does this mean?" Her eyes flickered speculatively to Karen.

"Not what you think it means," commented Karen dryly. "Paul wants to speak to you, Mother. He has a proposition to suggest."

"A proposition!" Madeline looked intrigued. Her life had been rather dull of late, and now this annoying business with Sandra had depressed her terribly. But this sounded exciting. Paul had always been so generous towards her. He understood her little ways. She smiled charmingly. "Well, what is it?" she prompted.

Karen looked at Sandra. "I think it would be as well if Sandra left us alone for a while," she said quietly. "Could you go to your room, honey, and play some records for five minutes?"

Sandra frowned. "Why should I do that?" she exclaimed angrily. "I'm not a child. What is it you have to say that I can't hear?"

Paul looked directly at her. "You'll be told soon enough. Just give us a few minutes alone with your mother, please."

Sandra responded to Paul's quiet injunction. He was at once gentle and reassuring and she had always wanted to please him before anyone else.

"Will it take long?" she asked pleadingly. "Is it about Simon?"

"Relax!" said Paul, his patience holding out.

"But are you going to split on me? Paul, you can't!" Her face was appealing. Begging him to go away and not say anything of what he had heard to her mother.

"Don't worry," said Paul, his voice a little harder. "Whatever I have to say to your mother is for your own good."

Sandra's face changed. "You're all the same," she cried, tears beginning to overflow her eyes. "You all hate me. You don't want me to be happy."

"That's enough," said Paul, his voice now as cold as

ice. "Go to your room, Sandra, and stay there until you're sent for."

Sandra flounced out, slamming the door behind her, and they heard her footsteps as she ran sobbing up the stairs.

Madeline looked reproachfully at Paul. "Poor Sandra," she said. "You were always her hero. You've really broken faith with her."

"Sandra needed firm handling years ago," retorted Paul, offering Karen a cigarette. "Shall we sit down?"

"Of course. Do forgive me." Madeline turned off the television and Karen subsided on to an armchair. Paul himself sat down on the couch, leaning forward, legs apart, his fingers toying with his cigarette. Karen looked at him and felt her heart contract. No man should affect her the way that Paul affected her. Just looking at him caused the bones in her body to melt away and gave her an insatiable desire to touch him.

As if Paul was conscious of her scrutiny, he looked at her just then, and for a moment their eyes met. She was forced to look away first; she was afraid of the emotion he might see in her eyes.

She drew on her cigarette. What did he really think of this affair? What did he really think of her mother? Of Sandra?

"Well, Mother," began Karen awkwardly, taking the first plunge, "Sandra has still been trying to see Simon."

"What?" Madeline was horrified. "Are you sure?"

"Of course we're sure," said Karen, with a brief glance at Paul.

Madeline frowned, her face deepening in colour. "But you told me ..." she began, angrily.

Paul interrupted the tirade which was about to start.

"Before you say any more, Madeline, I suggest you hear what else there is to hear."

Madeline flushed deeper. "That's all very well, but I thought Karen had spoken to you about this earlier on."

"So she did," exclaimed Paul. "It's not been so successful, however. Your darling teenager has been writing passionate letters to Simon and telephoning him. She even went so far as to ring him at his home and Julia began complaining."

Madeline was flabbergasted. That her little Sandra should act in such a shameless way was positively stunning. She had never grown beyond the stage of seeing Sandra as a child with dolls and dolls' prams, playing in the street, her fair chubbiness making her the envy of all the mothers round about.

She now pressed a hand to her mouth. "Oh no!" she groaned, half disbelievingly. "How could she do such a thing? Degrading herself like that!"

"Mother, please," exclaimed Karen, sighing. "Don't be hysterical."

"Me? Hysterical?" gasped Mrs. Stacey wildly. "How can you talk like that? How can you be so complacent about it? Your own sister involved with a married man! I'm sorry, Paul, but you know what a waster Simon is. As for you, Karen, have you no feelings? I believe you don't care about us at all. You and your independence! A fine mess both you and Sandra are making of your lives."

Karen flushed and looked uncomfortably at Paul. What must he be thinking? she wondered. Until now, her mother had always behaved with the utmost decorum in his presence. This spate of wild accusations must be a revelation to him.

In truth, Paul was astounded at Madeline's attempts to put the whole blame of the situation on Karen. After all, she had really no one to blame but herself.

"Madeline," he said distinctly, "Karen has no part in this, no part at all. You are to blame. You spoiled Sandra all her life, brought her up to believe she could have anything she wanted. Now that she finds life isn't all a bed of roses, she's taking it hard!"

Madeline was taken aback. Until now only Karen had ever criticized her in this way. "Sandra is only a child!" she exclaimed tearfully. "I'm sure I've only tried to do my best for her. I am her mother, you know. She hardly knew her father. If I've indulged her a little –"

"Oh, let's at least be honest!" Paul was blunt. "You've ruined Sandra and I doubt very much that either of you could change at this late date." He ignored Madeline's imploring eyes. "I want to help you, not merely for Sandra's sake, but for Simon, too. I put a suggestion to Karen this afternoon which she agrees might help to solve the problem. It was she who thought we ought to hear your reactions before acting upon it."

Mrs. Stacey wiped her eyes dramatically. "You're not thinking of taking Sandra away from me?" she implored.

"Of course not, Mother," cried Karen exasperatedly. "We're not inhuman!"

Madeline sniffed. "Go on, then, Paul."

"It's simply this." Paul sighed. "You and Sandra leave London, for a few weeks. You go away and take a holiday in the sun together, and Sandra will doubtless forget all about Simon in the search for more, shall we say, local talent. Naturally, I will take it upon myself to pay all your expenses, plus some spending money."

Madeline's eyes grew rounder every second and Karen thought, half disgustedly, that the money involved meant nothing to her mother as long as she was going to enjoy herself. She even wondered whether Sandra was really considered in those first few minutes after Paul's announcement.

"Why, Paul!" she cried at last. "What a wonderful idea! I don't know how to thank you. It seems an ideal solution."

Paul looked rather cynical. Karen realized that he knew just how strong was the power of money in almost anything. Madeline had been revealed as a keen contestant in the money-grabbing stakes and her feelings for Sandra were secondary by comparison.

"I gather you're agreeable," remarked Paul softly.

"But of course!" said Madeline excitedly, mentally imagining herself away from the rather polluted atmosphere of London at the moment. "Karen, my dear, forgive me. This is a wonderful solution. And here was I, imagining that you didn't care about us."

"It's Paul idea," replied Karen dryly. "Don't thank me. I had nothing to do with it."

Madeline made a teasing face at her elder daughter, but Karen refused to respond to the open invitation. She felt she had had enough of her mother for one evening.

Paul looked intently at Karen for a moment, noticing her rather strained expression. He could understand her feelings. She had been all for refusing his offer and managing on her own. To find her mother overjoyed at the prospect of what was, for her, a free holiday could not be pleasing.

He drew on his cigarette and exhaled the blue smoke into the air with slow deliberation. Then he said thoughtfully:

"I suggest you go to Spain. It's very pleasant there at this time of the year."

Karen gasped. "Spain!" she echoed in amazement, ignoring her mother's exhilarated expression. "Paul, I was under the impression that you meant somewhere in the south of England, maybe the west coast or something."

Paul shrugged his broad shoulders. "A holiday? In England at this time of the year?" he said, his voice amused. "My dear Karen, there would be no pleasure in sea fronts and high winds and watery sunshine."

"No, indeed," exclaimed Madeline, twisting her fingers together in anticipation. "Oh, Paul, what a wonderful trip this will be!"

Paul flicked the ash from his cigarette into the fire.

"Good," he said easily. "And now I suggest wc allow you to tell Sandra yourself. I think it will probably be as well if you ignore the fact of Sandra meeting Simon recently and merely suggest a holiday because your health has been rather poor lately and I agreed to finance you.

It's rather thin, I know, but once you're away from here, lazing on the Costa Brava, you will find that Sandra is much more amiable towards the idea."

"All right, Paul. You know best. I'm sure Sandra will soon find herself another boy-friend once we are away from your brother. Until now she has seemed quite satisfied with boys of her own age. I can only assume that Simon encouraged her quite outrageously."

Karen rose to her feet, her face unsmiling.

"I think we'll go, Mother," she said coolly. "You can let me know if you want anything. If you have any problems." This last sounded quite sarcastic, but she couldn't help it. Her mother really was as transparent as glass, although at times the glass had two sides.

Madeline was too engrossed with her own thoughts to pay much heed to Karen's expression. She merely nodded and looked up at Paul.

Paul himself strolled to the door. "By the way," he remarked, "I'll have my secretary fix up the details with you, hotels, air tickets, etc. We will fix the accommodation and you will simply have to obtain passports for yourself and Sandra. Could you be ready to leave in a week?"

"Oh, I should think so. Yes!" exclaimed Madeline, standing up also now. "Paul darling, I do want to thank you for this, most fervently."

"It's nothing," said Paul abruptly, and opened the lounge door. He took his own and Karen's coat from the hall closet, which he remembered from his days of being married to Karen, and helped her on with hers. As he slipped the garment on to her shoulders allowing her to slide in her arms, he reflected that it was quite like old times here. They had visited her mother quite regularly, although many times it had just been a duty visit. He remembered how they had enjoyed getting home again after listening to a monologue from Madeline about the afternoon's bridge party, and how they had removed their coats and flung themselves down in front of the fire in the lounge of Trevayne, and talked about things in general until the early hours, happy just being alone together.

How great was the transition from those days! How could he forgive Karen for ruining his life?

As they drove back to Karen's apartment, Paul said: "Have you had dinner?"

Karen looked at him in surprise. "No, why? I was going to go back home and have a snack."

Paul nodded and said: "Would you have dinner with me, then?"

Karen's eyes widened. "If you like," she agreed, smiling a little. "What am I to be? A stop-gap?"

Paul sounded amused himself. "My dear Karen, you couldn't be called that by any stretch of the imagination. No ... I'm free for the rest of the evening and so are you, so why don't we spend it together?"

"Why, indeed?" she remarked dryly, but inwardly her heart was dancing. At least an evening in his company was something.

They drove out of London to a roadhouse called the Ebony Cane.

It was near Maidstone and Karen had never even heard of the place, but as they crossed the threshold into the pile-carpeted hall she was very impressed by the luxurious décor and glamorous hostesses. The furniture too had been designed to suit the place, with ebony-legged tables and vases of flowers shaped like walking-sticks. The lighting was brilliant and counterbalanced the almost overwhelming black and white effect of everything. Black carpets and sparkling white damask table covers, black chairs with soft white seats, and the hostesses in black and white outfits of bodice and tights, with white aprons which gave a mock-businesslike effect.

The manager himself attended to Paul, recognizing him immediately, and although the room was crowded, strings were pulled and a table for two was found in a secluded alcove.

Karen removed her coat and slipped into the seat the manager held for her while Paul ordered Martinis and picked up the menu. He studied it for a moment and then Karen said:

"You seem quite well known here."

He smiled amiably. "I should be," he remarked casually. "The company owns the place."

Karen's eyes widened in surprise. "I didn't know they dabbled in the catering field."

"They don't normally. It's a try-out of an idea. We designed the layout, and if it pays off we should get a lot of publicity from it."

Karen nodded approvingly. "Very clever," she said, shrugging her slim shoulders. "And I suppose it was your idea?"

Paul grinned. "How did you guess?" He looked fully at her. "Are you hungry?"

"Not particularly, I'm afraid. Why? Did you design the menu as well?"

Paul smiled. "*Touché*," he murmured. "Shall I order?"

"With pleasure," replied Karen. "You'll know all the nicest things."

"Not only about food," he remarked dryly, an amused expression in his eye.

Karen flushed and was glad when the head waiter appeared to take their order. Paul chose a large assortment of dishes and Karen hoped she could do justice to them.

After he had ordered, they had cigarettes, and Karen allowed her gaze to wander around the room. She found that quite a few eyes turned their way and she wondered whether they were people who knew Paul. And if so, did they know her?

The contemporary style of the room was quite extraordinary and she could quite see many people talking about it and in turn bringing more people to the roadhouse.

"How long has the place been open?" she asked Paul curiously.

Paul shrugged. "I guess about two months," he replied smoothly. "Do you like it?"

Karen shrugged herself. "I like it, but it's way out, really. Do many people go for this kind of thing?"

Paul nodded. "Yes, I think so. That's why I was so impressed by your paintings. They have the same kind of stunning impact."

"Thank you." Karen smiled and turned her gaze to the small dais where a five-piece band played low music that formed a background to the buzz of conversation. There was a small cabaret floor and a microphone, and she assumed there would be guest artists later. The floor formed a small dance floor as well, and although there wasn't much room, she supposed people managed. After all, people didn't move much when they were dancing nowadays.

She returned her eyes to Paul, who was studying the wine list. He was unconscious of her gaze at the moment and she could study him unobtrusively. He looked as handsome as usual, his hair shining and his shirt sparkling whitely against the tan of his skin. A tan which he must have acquired earlier in the year, at winter sports, perhaps. He looked vitally masculine and she felt her heart contract painfully. How could she have left him those years ago? How did people drift into these things so that there was no going back? Pride was little comfort at times like this.

Was Ruth to be the guiding factor in his life from now on? Could she stand it to happen? Remembering Ruth's almost too-sweet features, she shivered involuntarily. Ruth could not make him really happy, she felt convinced of that. She was too young and babyish, too dependent, too clinging. Paul needed a woman who could meet him half-way. Who could talk to him as well as listen.

Suddenly she realized that he was aware of her scrutiny

and the ready flush stained her cheeks. He always seemed to catch her out in embarrassing situations, and she tried to make light of it by saying:

"You don't change much, Paul."

He looked cynical.

"I suppose I can take that as a compliment," he said, amused. "It could have a double meaning, but I'll give you the benefit of the doubt."

Karen felt small again. It had been ridiculous making such a pointless remark. He must be conscious that she had been trying to distract his attention from herself.

Leaning back in his seat, he said: "Tell me, have you done any more painting?"

She shook her head. "No. Why?"

Paul frowned. "Well, actually, I've thought a lot about them this week," he replied surprisingly. "And I should like a friend of mine to take a look at them. Aaron Bernard. Have you heard of him?"

"Aaron Bernard!" exclaimed Karen in astonishment. "But you must know he's one of the world's foremost art critics?"

"Precisely," said Paul easily. "He is also interested in discovering new talent. I think he would be fascinated by your work."

Karen looked sceptical. She remembered Lewis's comments and said:

"Oh, but Paul, Lewis knows a lot about art and he has no faith in me at all."

Paul's eyes grew cold.

"Indeed. And you would trust his word above mine, I suppose? If you want my opinion, I think Martin places far too much emphasis on his own judgment. What is he, after all? A textile designer with aspirations over and above his capabilities."

Karen's eyes widened.

"That's not exactly true, Paul. Lewis has been very helpful to me ever since ... the divorce."

"And beforehand, no doubt," retorted Paul angrily.

"God, Karen, don't try to sell the man to me! I have nothing to thank him for. It's only by a great effort of self-control that I force myself to even look at him. Believe me, he and I have nothing in common. I think I hate the man."

Karen sighed. "All right, Paul. I can understand your antagonism towards him, but speaking strictly objectively, he has quite good ideas usually."

Paul shrugged. "I still say he's wrong. And how in hell's name can I be objective about a man who has . . . well . . . seduced my wife?"

Karen flushed scarlet. "Oh, Paul, you surely don't still believe that he and I were once lovers!" she exclaimed.

Paul's face darkened ominously. "And why not? My God, Karen, I divorced you on that assumption. It was adultery, remember? If it wasn't true, why didn't you defend the suit?

Karen bit her lip. "And if I had? What good would it have done? Would you have believed me?"

"At that time, I think one grain of hope would have convinced me," he muttered harshly. "If you had once shown you wanted to come back, it would have made all the difference."

Karen clasped her fingers together. Why, oh, why had he said that? It made everything so awful; so senseless.

She was relieved of any need to answer when the soup was brought and although she now felt little like food she made a pretence of eating it. Paul did not seem very interested in the delicious-smelling consommé either, and when the waiter had departed again, he said:

"You forget that I was neatly supplied with proof. It seemed conclusive. Your silence made it so. Apart from anything else, Martin admitted it was true, every word of it."

"Nonsense!" exclaimed Karen furiously. "Lewis wouldn't say a thing like that. And if he did, how could you possibly be sure?"

"I had a lawyer, remember?" remarked Paul dryly.

"Everything is cut and dried to them. It was a simple enough case. What more was there to say? Anyway, forget it. It's not a pleasant topic to discuss with your dinner."

But Karen didn't want to forget it. Any of it. How could Lewis have admitted such a thing when they had never been anything more than friendly with each other? She was confused. She had thought Lewis was such a loyal and true friend, but within a short time he had been reduced to ... what? A liar? A strange and frightening menace?

She shrugged such thoughts away. There must be an explanation. He must have thought he was helping her by defending her. Had he said it was all his fault to exonerate her from all blame? And yet she was still unsatisfied. It was perplexing and frightening, and without Lewis there was no one to whom she could turn. No one to tell it all to ... to ask advice from ...

She determined to have it out with Lewis himself. After all, he might have a reasonable explanation. And if he denied it? Well, she would take that hurdle when it arose. Perhaps Paul had mistaken his meaning. Perhaps he had implied something that Paul had accepted as a fact because he expected it? She was searching wildly now. Clutching at straws as they say. but there had to be a reason. There was always a reason for everything.

She was silent for so long that the meal was far advanced before she spoke again, and then it was only in answer to Paul's words:

"Well," he said, "do you want Aaron Bernard to look at your paintings?"

"Do I want?" Karen roused herself from her reverie. "But of course, Paul, of course I want him to come. But only if you really think he won't be wasting his time. I think I should hate him to ridicule them once and for all. That would finish everything, and at the moment I always feel that strange hopefulness that one day I really will do something worth while. I've had my own enjoyment from them and if he said I really was a fool to continue then I should feel utterly depressed."

Paul smiled, relaxing. "I wish I could be as sure of everything as I am that I'm not mistaken in you." He sighed. "However, if he does dislike them, I myself will buy them from you."

Karen's eyes narrowed. "For your new home?" she asked mockingly.

"Maybe," he replied, raising his glass of wine to his lips, and looking at her over the rim. "Does that surprise you?"

"You must be joking," she exclaimed. "It positively astounds me. If I were Ruth I wouldn't want another woman's paintings in the house, especially not when the artist concerned was once my husband's wife." She laughed. "That sounds rather ridiculous, doesn't it?"

Paul's face had grown a little taut.

"A little," he agreed slowly. "But then, Karen, you're so much different from Ruth. She has not your, shall we say, dominating personality. You like to feel on equal terms with men; Ruth is quite prepared to remain a feminine counterpart. Intelligent, able to listen and understand her husband's conversation, but nevertheless, remaining completely absorbed with the home."

"Oh, my Gawd," exclaimed Karen, with a broad Cockney accent, quite unable to restrain her amusement. "The typical 'little woman'. Will she darn your socks, darling, and put your slippers by the fire for you?"

Paul's colour heightened slightly and she knew he was angry.

"At least she won't be interested in furthering her career," he snapped. "Ruth has never had to work, so she won't miss it." His voice was harsh. "Believe me, Karen, most women enjoy being a wife and mother in the true sense of the word."

Karen now looked embarrassed, but her words were coolly amused as he said:

"Oh, darling. I think you're really terribly old-fashioned at heart." She smiled wryly. "You want someone in satins and laces with frills and furbelows everywhere. I was much too depressingly plain and down to earth. And I committed the deadliest of sins, I answered back and expected to be listened to."

Paul's fingers were clenched round the slender stem of the wine glass, and Karen thought it was a miracle of design that it did not snap in two.

"You not only answered back," he said with deadly calm. "You left me, Karen. Never forget that. You . . . left . . . me. Just to prove you were as utterly independent as you had always said you were. To prove you were utterly unabsorbed with the job of being *Mrs. Paul Frazer.*"

Karen pushed away the dish of strawberry mousse which she had not touched.

"Yes, I did that, didn't I?" she said, laughing without humour. "Which just goes to prove that even I am not infallible."

Paul's face hardened.

"You don't really believe that," he said coldly. "I suppose it simply amuses you to taunt me."

"Amuses me?" Karen looked astounded. "I can assure you that that episode in my life is not my most memorable, unpleasant though it was."

"Then what was?" he asked, his curiosity overwhelming his natural restraint.

"Our honeymoon, I think." she answered, looking down at her coffee, which was now going cold.

Paul did not reply. He merely produced his cigarette case and they lit cigarettes in silence.

"This is really quite an amusing situation, if you think about it," Karen said suddenly. "Here we are, two divorced people, sitting here having dinner together as though we were old friends. Lord, what a distance civilization has come! We seem to have lost all the primitive emotions in the cauldron of neutrality, or should I say respectability. There's no red blood any more. Only this kind of half-hearted tolerance which does away with healthy antagonism."

"Profound words," remarked Paul with a cynical smile. "Shall we go on that note?"

They accomplished the drive back to Berkshire Court in a rather strained and tense atmosphere. When Paul stopped outside the block of apartments, Karen looked reflectively at him. His profile gave nothing away, and she switched on the interior light to see him more clearly.

"Well," she said lightly, trying to resume the rather bantering tone on which the evening had begun, "thank you for all you've done for me and for Mother and Sandra. You've proved you really are a gentleman after all." Her voice was infinitely mocking, but Paul's face remained impassive.

In the dull light the colour of Karen's hair gleamed like silver against the creamy colour of the mohair coat and as she moved her head, the silky strands brushed the shoulder of his overcoat. She was so cool, so lovely and so challenging, and Paul felt his senses stirring rapidly. It was infuriating to find himself responding to her as before, particularly after all she had said, after all that was between them.

"Good night," he said pointedly, his lean hands gripping the wheel until the knuckles grew white. He did not know how long he could control himself.

Karen, not understanding, shrugged and opened the car door.

"Good night," she said, and slid out.

Paul did not speak again. He merely nodded, switched out the interior light and then sent the car away as fast as the wheels would take him. The rear wheels almost spun in his haste, and Karen watched him turn on to the main road before walking into the apartments. She felt alone and cold and strangely scared of the future, but what had frightened her she could not say.

CHAPTER SIX

The following week passed slowly. Karen's mother rang to say that Sandra seemed to be accepting the fact of going away, although she had shown very little enthusiasm. Karen was not worried. She felt sure that once Sandra was away from the influence of Simon she would revert to her old, if rather annoying, self. After all, a holiday in Spain would please anybody and Sandra was still a child whatever way you looked at it, and her emotions could not seriously be involved. It seemed that the episode was almost over, for after Madeline and Sandra left for the Costa Brava there would be no further need to see Paul. And anyway, his marriage was looming on the horizon, getting nearer every day.

She went into the office and saw Lewis, hoping he would have reverted also to his normal, amiable manner, but he still remained in that curiously half-threatening mood and Karen could not understand him. She half believed it was her own disturbed mind that was creating the impression of Lewis being different, but she seriously began thinking about taking another job.

She began studying the "situations vacant" columns in the newspapers, but nothing seemed to interest her. Still, she argued, there was no hurry, and as she had worked for Lewis for so long she could surely work a little longer.

And then, towards the end of the week, she was awakened one morning by the shrilling of the telephone. She rolled lazily over in bed, her head throbbing at the sudden rousing from the deep sleep she had been in. She had had to take a sleeping pill the night before to get to sleep at all, and the effects were hardly wearing off. She focused her eyes on the clock with difficulty. Seven-fifteen! Who on earth could be ringing her at this ungodly hour! Blinking, she sat up, shaking her head to banish the sleep from her eyes. She slid slowly out of bed, pulling on her quilted housecoat. Opening the lounge door, she walked lazily over to the telephone. Mrs. Coates had not yet arrived so she supposed it might be her ringing to say she could not come. But then Mrs. Coates would know she would still be in bed and would hardly ring so early.

Lifting the scarlet receiver, she said: "Yes, who is it?"

"Karen? Karen, is that you at last?"

Karen blinked rapidly. It was her mother's urgent voice.

"Good lord, Mother," she exclaimed, "who else did you expect at this address?" She sounded amused.

"Don't be facetious," replied Madeline promptly, her voice shaky.

"Seriously though, Mother, what goes on? Do you realize the time?"

"Yes, yes, yes, of course I do. Karen, this is very important. Pull yourself together, do." There was a pause and Karen thought she heard her sobbing softly to herself.

"Well, go on," she exclaimed. A cold hand was clutching her stomach. Something serious must have happened. "What is it?" she exclaimed impatiently. "Is it Sandra? Is she hurt?"

"Worse than that," replied Madeline, her voice breaking. "She's run away and left me a note. She says she's going to have a baby. Simon Frazer's baby."

"Oh, lord!" Karen sank down on to the couch beside the telephone. "What a mess! All right, Mother, you just stay right there and relax. I'll be straight over. It won't take me long. Make some coffee or something."

"All right, Karen. But be quick. I can't bear this alone."

Madeline rang off and Karen clasped her hands together apprehensively. What a thing to happen! Just as she had thought everything was working out nicely. The crazy little idiot! Allowing this to happen. Allowing

Simon to even get that near her.

She rose to her feet restlessly. A baby! What could they do now? Simon would not be very pleased, she felt sure of that, whatever Sandra thought he felt for her. He wanted nothing so much as freedom, and babies spelt responsibilities.

Forcing herself to act swiftly, she dressed in dark blue slacks and an Italian over-blouse of bright yellow. She pulled on her sheepskin coat and left the apartment. She drove round to her mother's home in her own car and parked it outside.

The door was opened at her approach and her mother was waiting in the hall. She was still wearing her dressing-gown, and rollers were in her hair. She flung herself rather dramatically at Karen and there followed a paroxysm of weeping and self-recriminations before she controlled herself sufficiently to allow Karen to draw her into the sitting-room. The electric heater was burning and Liza had arranged a tray of coffee on a low table.

Karen deliberately poured two cups of coffee, handed one to her mother and then said:

"Right. What happened?" She sipped her coffee appreciatively, feeling some of the chill leaving her body.

Madeline bit her lip, restraining the ready tears.

"Well, when Sandra and I discussed this trip abroad I told you she didn't seem over-enthusiastic, didn't I?"

"Yes."

"Apparently she was planning this all the time. I assume that beast knows all about it, though."

"Simon?"

"Who else? He must have put her up to it, leaving me, I mean."

"That doesn't sound like Simon," remarked Karen dryly. "He's hardly the type to go for this sort of thing. In my opinion, this has all been Sandra's idea, and probably Simon doesn't even know."

"Who else would she tell?" retorted her mother, and Karen thought there might be some truth in that. "Oh,

I told Sandra we were going abroad for me as much as for her, but she hardly believed me, I'm sure. She knew we were trying to separate her from that man and she didn't like it. And for good reason as it turns out. Oh, Sandra!" She dissolved into tears again.

Karen lit a cigarette. Things were bad enough without her mother losing complete control of herself. Madeline composed herself after a while and went on:

"I shouldn't have known yet, but I woke up at five-thirty with a terrible headache. I had no aspirin so I went into Sandra's room to see if she had, and then I found her bed empty ... and the note pinned to her pillow."

Karen sighed heavily. "And have her clothes gone?"

"Some of them. She could have gone at any time really. She said she was going to bed at nine o'clock because she felt so tired. I went about ten-thirty and I did not look to see if she was all right, so she might have been gone then."

"I see. And what did you do when you found the note?"

"I rang you, of course."

"But it was seven o'clock before you contacted me."

"I rang and rang," replied her mother, sobbing. "I couldn't get any reply. I thought you must be away."

The sleeping pill, thought Karen. "I'm sorry," she said. "I must have been sleeping heavily."

"You must indeed," exclaimed her mother, frowning. "Anyway," she felt in her dressing-gown pocket, "here's the note."

Karen opened it. It said simply:

Dear Mum,

My life here has become intolerable. You and Karen are determined to separate me from the one man I love, and I can't stand it. I'm expecting Simon's baby and we expect to be married as soon as that awful Julia gets a divorce. Don't try to find me. I'll come back when you realize I'm right.

Sandra.

"The little bitch," muttered Karen angrily. "If I could get my hands on her at this moment I'd ... Who does she think she is, anyway? And how can she afford to go away at all?"

"Her Post Office Savings Bank book has gone," replied Madeline dully. "She had about seventy-five pounds in that, I think."

"That won't last long," remarked Karen practically. "How dare she act so thoughtlessly!"

"It's probably my fault," cried Madeline, tears coursing down her cheeks again. "I never have tried to understand her problems."

Karen privately agreed that it was Madeline's fault, but not for those reasons.

"For goodness' sake, Mother," she exclaimed, "you know very well you have always tried to understand Sandra. That's her trouble. She gets too much understanding. She needs a damn good hiding."

"Oh, Karen, don't be so hard! Sandra was always much more my daughter than you ever were. You couldn't possibly understand the relationship we shared."

"Some relationship," remarked Karen coldly. "I'm sorry, Mother, but you have only yourself to blame."

"Thank you." Madeline wiped her eyes. "Why did you come here? To torture me or to help me?"

"To help you, of course," exclaimed Karen. "Don't let's quarrel, Mother. We're in this together, whatever you may think. I simply don't want you to imagine that Sandra is a poor, misunderstood teenager. She's simply a spoilt, irresponsible, self-centred child and she needs a firm hand, not a gentle one."

"But to be pregnant! Oh, Karen, whatever will we do?"

"Don't panic!" exclaimed Karen, sounding calmer herself than she felt. "Try and relax, Mother. There must be something we can do."

Her mother looked bleakly at her. "There is. You can call Paul and tell him."

Karen clenched her fists. Deep inside her she knew that Paul was the only person likely to help them. Was it fair to him to expect him to help them again?

"I know," said Karen slowly. "I suppose that is the only sensible thing to do, but I think it's rather putting on him, don't you?"

Madeline rose to her feet. "If it weren't for his brother there would be no problem." she replied, with dignity.

"Well, all right," said Karen, sighing. She walked out into the hall where the telephone was installed. It was still not much after eight, so she dialled the number of his apartment in Belgravia.

The low tone seemed to ring for ages before a click showed that the receiver had been lifted. A moment later a lazy, husky voice answered, Paul's voice.

"Frazer here," he said, his voice still drowsy with sleep.

"Paul, this is Karen."

"Karen?" There was silence for a moment as though he was sitting up in bed before going on. "God, do you know what time it is?"

"Yes, but this is important. Can I see you?"

"Now?"

"Unless you'd rather I told you over the phone. In fact that might be best."

"No, no." Paul sounded firm. "I'll see you. Where are you?"

"I'm at Mother's. Will you come over?"

Paul hesitated a moment and then he said:

"You come here instead. By the time I get dressed and shaved you could be here."

"All right, Paul. Thanks." She rang off and went back to her mother. "I'm going over to Paul's apartment. He's not up yet and I can be there by the time he's shaved and dressed."

"Oh." Mrs. Stacey looked perturbed. "You won't forget the reason why you're going, will you?"

Karen looked exasperated. "Honestly, Mother, you

are the absolute limit! The reason I'm going at all is because of you, isn't it?"

"Well ... yes, I suppose so."

"Then what do you mean by saying such a thing? Really, it's ridiculous."

Her mother had the grace to look ashamed. "I just thought that Paul is a very attractive man and you were once ... well ..."

Karen pulled on her coat again. "I'll be back later," she said abruptly, and left the house.

She drove swiftly towards Paul's apartment. The roads were already getting busy and traffic jams held her up causing her to inwardly fume and wish she had taken a taxi. They always seemed to get away quicker. She reached Ambleford House by eight-forty. The forecourt of the luxurious block of apartments was ready buzzing with cars, chauffeur-driven, many of them, waiting for the affluent occupants of the apartments in the building.

Inside, the gleaming chrome-plated lifts were all in operation and she had to wait impatiently for one to reach the ground floor. Out came a couple of bespectacled men in city suits and bowlers, canes tucked under their arms. She half smiled at their swift appraisal of herself in the casual slacks and sheepskin coat. She obviously did not look the type that usually visited the apartment. She was conscious of their regard, but slipped easily into the lift and pressed the button for the top floor where Paul's penthouse was situated.

She rode up nervously now. As she neared the apartment she was forced to realize just how much had happened since she last used this lift. The corridor when she stepped out on to it was pile-carpeted, and the door at the end had Paul's name on it instead of giving a number.

The apartment had a panoramic view of the city of London and Karen had always adored it. She and Paul had often slept there in the old days after spending a night in town. They could be completely alone with no one to disturb them, and as the thoughts came back to Karen they were disturbing in themselves.

She shivered involuntarily as she rang the bell and waited to be admitted. A manservant opened the door, one she did not recognize, so she presumed Paul must have dismissed the old staff and engaged new ones.

She felt strangely disappointed. She had half expected Paul to be alone and to find this man here proved it was not to be so. She ought to have realized that Paul would need someone to prepare his meals and serve at table if he had guests for a meal.

She stepped inside and was immediately re-enamoured of the lounge. It was empty, and she moved slowly across to the window which stretched almost completely along one wall. The view was exactly as she remembered it, the vista a delight to behold. Up here, the sounds of London were muted to a murmur. The manservant informed her that Mr. Frazer was in the shower and would be out directly, and then disappeared through the door leading to the kitchen.

Karen turned back and surveyed the room with pleasure. The contemporary Swedish furniture was light and attractive, the white leather couches showing up to advantage against the rich red of the carpet. The walls were covered in murals of Norway which Paul had had done at her request after they had spent a holiday there. The room was centrally heated, as were all the apartments, and a librenza separated the dining recess from the rest of the room. It was quite a large recess, and was well able to accommodate half a dozen people for a meal. The whole place was filled with memories for Karen and nostalgia welled up inside her. She wished she had not had to come, but had she refused it would have looked extremely odd. After all, places were what you made them, and just because once she had been happy here was no reason to avoid it.

The apartment had two bedrooms with adjoining bathrooms, a kitchen and a study, and this large lounge.

The staff who worked in the apartments of the whole block were accommodated in self-contained flats in the basement so that although they could be reached from above they had homes completely their own. Consequently, the tenants of the apartments found no difficulty in finding staff.

Extracting a cigarette from an ebony case on a low table, Karen lit it and removed her sheepskin coat. It was warm in the apartment after the chilly morning air outside. She felt herself relaxing a little and sighed.

Wandering round restlessly, waiting for Paul, she examined the ornaments without interest, lifting books from their shelves and replacing them again. She barely registered the titles of the books before so doing.

When she had finished her cigarette, she stubbed it out in an ashtray and on impulse crossed to the door leading in to the master bedroom. She was curious to see whether he had changed its appearance, and besides, it was the room they had used to use. The huge bed was unmade, the covers rumpled from Paul's occupation. Obviously the manservant had not yet found time to make it. Apart from the bed the room was immaculately neat, the cream carpet underfoot was as soft as she remembered, although dark rugs had been added, making the room appear more masculine. The bed-head was quilted in dark blue brocade, and the hangings at the windows were yellow, hand-painted linen. The furniture was a darker wood and gave the room a restful air. Karen had always liked it, and her opinion had not altered. The room now smelt of tobacco and after-shave lotion, and that certain maleness that proved there was no woman in the apartment.

Karen crossed to the window and opened it wide, leaning out. The gardens of Ambleford House lay below and were rich with daffodils and tulips. She sighed regretfully. How strange was life, or was it fate? A few weeks ago she had never dreamed she would ever speak to Paul again. She had thought everything was finished.

Today she was surrounded by his possessions, standing here in the apartment, in his bedroom of all places. She smiled. What strange things happened; how much stranger than fiction was this whole business.

There was suddenly the sound of a door opening behind her, the door from the adjoining bathroom. Paul entered the bedroom and Karen swung round feeling foolishly childish at having been caught out, like a child at the forbidden biscuit tin.

He was dressed only in dark trousers and his dark hair was ruffled. His broad, tanned chest was bare, a towel about his neck.

Karen blushed in confusion, feeling suddenly very embarrassed. What on earth would he read into this? What a fool she was. Her eyes flickered over him; she saw the thick covering of dark hair on his chest, the narrowness of his hips, and felt the compulsive masculinity of his whole being. His eyes were dark and inscrutable and were watching her closely. If he was surprised to see her he gave no sign, and after a moment he said:

"I'm sorry I wasn't waiting for you when you arrived. You must forgive me. I was rather tired. I was working late last night."

"That's all right." Karen gathered her scattered wits. Seeing him, so dear and handsome, had almost caused her to give herself away. For a moment, all thoughts of Sandra and her mother were forgotten, and she wanted to fling herself into his arms. "I . . . er . . . I was just looking around," she finished lamely.

Paul reached into a drawer for a clean white shirt and put it on slowly and deliberately, fastening the buttons and thrusting it into his trousers.

"That's all right," he said lazily, "you've not offended me."

Karen's flushed deepened and she said, "Oh!" in an irritated voice, and after slamming the window shut she marched back into the lounge, aware of his amused gaze following her. He really was the limit, standing there dressing himself as though he did it every day of his life, in front of her.

Paul followed her, and Karen forced herself to act naturally and sank down on to a low couch. She reached for a cigarette, and after he had lit it for her she said abruptly:

"Sandra has run away. She says she's expecting a baby. And you can guess whose it is."

Paul's rather amused expression changed rapidly.

"What!" he exclaimed angrily.

"She's written Mother a note saying she's pregnant," repeated Karen, drawing on her cigarette.

"My God!" Paul was absolutely astounded. He had never dreamed that Simon would go this far with a teenager like Sandra. He felt as though he could willingly strangle his brother at that moment. He ran a restless hand through his short, dark hair and turned away exasperatedly.

He walked across to the window and lit himself a cigarette.

Just then the manservant returned.

"Would you like some coffee, sir?" he asked politely.

"What ... oh, yes ... I suppose so, Travers, thank you," he said swinging round, and the man departed again.

Karen crossed her legs. "I'm sorry, Paul, but there was no one else to turn to but you. What can we do?"

Paul shook his head. "Don't perturb yourself on my account," he muttered. "Simon is to blame here, and he is just as much my concern as Sandra is yours, ridiculously enough." He ground his teeth together. "What a blasted idiot he is ... or words more fitted to this situation. Hell ... what on earth was Sandra thinking about? She must be mad!"

Karen shrugged, lying back against the soft upholstery.

"You'd better read the letter. It makes everything very clear ... except where she's gone."

She handed over the note and Paul swiftly scanned its contents.

"God, and she really believes he intends to divorce Julia! Why, it's not long ago that he told me he had no intention of doing any such thing."

"Do you think he's been meeting her again in secret?"

Paul shook his head. "I sent Simon to Nottingham last weekend. He only got back yesterday."

"Good. That means it's Sandra's idea. But the fact that she left it this long may be significant. Do you think she contacted Simon yesterday when he got back?"

"That's a remote possibility," admitted Paul slowly. "But whether he was sympathetic or not puzzles me. After all, he knows what I told him. I don't think Simon would be keen to break his word. He's not all bad, you know."

Karen shrugged. "So what happens now?"

"Well, we have got to find Sandra, and when we do . . . we'll face that contingency when it arises. I've got a few words to say to her myself."

Karen's eyes widened. Paul's face was grim and she was sure he meant what he said.

"And the baby?" she murmured softly.

"Would you want her to marry Simon if she could?" he asked bluntly.

Karen shook her head.

"Well then, she will simply have to go away and have the baby and then have it adopted. It sounds cruel, but what else is there?"

"You're right," said Karen, sighing. "But how are we going to find her?"

"I'll contact Simon, of course, and see if he knows where she has gone. It's possible that she's told him even if he wasn't keen on the idea."

"The thing is," said Karen slowly, "if Sandra were to stop and really think what she's done she would want to retract it, I'm sure. After all, she has her whole life ahead of her and this won't help her. It means giving up her job at the salon when she was just going to take leave of absence. Jobs like that are not easy to come by, and I believe she was doing quite well at her work."

"I know, and I agree with you. That's why I'm willing to help her even though she barely deserves it."

Travers came back with the tray of coffee and for a while there was silence as Karen poured out the steaming liquid and Paul pulled on his jacket. He informed Travers that they would both have breakfast in fifteen minutes, and Travers withdrew politely.

Karen looked speculatively at Paul. "I am staying for breakfast?" she said, rather surprised.

"Of course. It's no use running around without food. You look pale enough as it is."

"I do feel rather empty," she admitted with a smile. "It's quite like old times, breakfasting together."

Paul shrugged and buttoned his jacket. He looked cool and dependable, his mind already working ahead to the day's activities. Karen was eternally grateful that she had Paul to turn to. Without him the situation would seem black indeed. For how could her mother be expected to pay for Sandra to go away to have the baby? And Mrs. Stacey was not the sort of woman to want her neighbours to know what had happened to Sandra. She would be unable to live it down, and Karen could imagine the gossip hurting her mother more than anything. No, Paul had become the fairy godfather as far as the Staceys were concerned, and she wished she could tell him just how she felt.

"Do you find things much the same here then?" he asked, looking down at her.

"Yes. I still think it's a wonderful apartment."

"Why did you go into the bedroom?" he asked abruptly, and saw the colour stain her cheeks yet again.

"I was curious," she said defensively. "I was simply renewing my memories of the place."

"I see. And were they pleasant memories?"

"Naturally," she murmured lightly, not wanting to

get in too deeply and not wanting to start an argument either.

He smiled at her wryly. "At times you really are transparent," he said significantly.

"Am I? What do you mean?" she exclaimed, her eyes wary.

He shrugged. "Nothing, nothing, forget it."

But Karen could not forget it as easily as that. She felt affronted at the implied force behind his words, and she walked restlessly to the window. His barbed comments had set her nerves on edge and she wished she had not given him scope for his criticisms.

"Calm down," he said, half amused by her. "Don't take life so seriously."

Karen swung round and would have spoken but Travers reappeared. He had brought their breakfast of cereal, ham and eggs, toast and coffee, and they seated themselves in the recess. Paul ate quite a good breakfast, but Karen refused the cereal and fried food and merely ate a slice of toast and drank three cups of the delicious continental coffee.

Forcing herself to treat him in the same casual manner in which he treated her, she said:

"And when does Ruth get back from America?"

"Within the next day or so," replied Paul smoothly. "When last she telephoned me she said she would be home soon."

"And have you missed her?"

"Of course." He smiled. "She said she would cable her date and time of arrival, but since that phone call I've heard nothing."

"I see. You must feel quite excited to know she'll soon be here." Karen's voice was mocking now.

"Quite," he answered, an amused smile playing round his mouth.

They finished breakfast and suddenly Paul said:

"I nearly forgot to tell you, Karen. Aaron Bernard is interested in seeing your paintings."

Karen's eyes widened. "Honestly? Have you contacted him?"

"Yes. A couple of days ago. I intended ringing you yesterday morning but I was too busy and I had to get my work done. Then when I did ring last night I could get no reply."

The sleeping pill again!

"I see," she said. "Well, I took a sleeping pill about nine-thirty last night so if you rang after that..."

"I did," he said, frowning. "It was nearly ten o'clock when I rang. But what the hell are you doing taking sleeping tablets?"

"To keep awake," remarked Karen sardonically. "Why else?"

"Then stop it!" he ordered bluntly. "If you can't sleep there must be something troubling you. What is it?"

"Who are you?" she exclaimed mockingly, "the lonely hearts columnist?"

"No. Don't be so clever, Karen. I simply don't like to think of you taking drugs. In no time at all you need two tablets to sleep, and then three. Where does it end? You become completely reliant upon them."

"Yes, sir." Karen's meek voice did not amuse him, and he rose from the table looking annoyed. "Anyway," she said, "do go on about Aaron Bernard. When does he want to see the paintings?"

She followed Paul out of the recess and he lit his cigarette before answering. "He would like to see them today, actually," replied Paul quietly. "That's why I tried to get you last night."

"Oh, I see," Karen bit her lip. "I suppose that's out now?" She sounded as regretful as she felt.

"Not necessarily," answered Paul. "If I can arrange for him to come round late this afternoon that should be all right, shouldn't it?"

"But with all this bother over Sandra I don't know whether I should," she began, a little nervously.

"Nonsense," replied Paul coldly. "Good heavens, girl,

Sandra seems quite willing to take care of her own affairs. After all, even if she's pregnant, she's certainly not the first or the last girl to whom this has happened."

"*If* she's pregnant," echoed Karen. "Can there be any doubt?"

"I should say it was possible, if not very probable," said Paul dryly. "I don't think everything is just so, simply because Sandra says so. If nothing else, it could be a false alarm, couldn't it?"

"Oh, yes. I suppose so. But if she's done this as a stunt ..." Her voice trailed away. Surely that could not be possible, whatever Paul might say. Sandra couldn't be so cruel, after all Madeline has done for her.

"Well, I'll contact Aaron this morning and arrange a time, etc. We may have solved the 'Sandra' mystery by then, and if so, what could be a more enjoyable ending to the day?"

"You're right," she agreed, sighing. "Thank you, Paul."

Paul glanced at his watch. "It's nine-thirty," he said thoughtfully. "Simon is rarely in the office before ten, and goodness knows where he is at this moment. I wouldn't bet that he's at the flat, his and Julia's, I mean. If Sandra has sprung the unhappy tidings on him I'd like to bet he's in a blue funk at this moment."

"Well, I really ought to be going," began Karen, frowning. "Mother will be worried too, and she told me not to be long."

Paul shrugged and offered her a cigarette. "Relax," he said easily. "Hell, you're doing what she asked, aren't you?"

"I know, but ..."

"But nothing. Now, sit down and take it easy."

"Well, I'd better ring Mother."

"I'll ring your mother," said Paul decisively. "If there's anything to be said she can say it to me personally."

"She's probably having hysterics," said Karen worriedly.

"Rubbish!" said Paul dryly. "Your mother puts on a good act. She won't be so concerned if she thinks you're doing the worrying for her."

He pushed Karen on to the couch and lifted the receiver of the cream telephone beside him. He dialled the Stacey home and waited for Mrs. Stacey to answer.

Madeline was pleased to hear from Paul. It proved that Paul was dealing with the situation and as Paul had so astutely observed, when Madeline passed her troubles on to somebody else she immediately felt easier. She had always needed someone to cling to and today Paul was filling the bill. Paul told her to relax and go back to bed if she still felt unwell. He and Karen would find Sandra and bring her home. He was charmingly tactful and reassuring and Karen could imagine how thrilled her mother would be. Paul rang off with an injunction for her to take things easy, then turned smiling to Karen.

"You see," he said, amused, "she was quite lucid and amiable."

"Because it was you who rang. She adores you, or hadn't you guessed?"

"Me . . . or my influence?" remarked Paul cynically. "Does it worry you?"

"Not at all," replied Karen lightly, drawing on her cigarette. "By the way, you make finding Sandra sound like an easy exercise. Does nothing ever get you down?"

Paul's smile disappeared. "Only erring wives," he said cruelly.

Karen shivered. There was always the personal angle between them. So close to the surface was it that it emerged at every turning.

"What about unkind husbands?" said Karen, retaliating.

"Was I unkind?" he asked mockingly. "I think not."

"You're only thinking of the emotional angle," she replied softly.

"What other angle is there?"

"I'm a person, not a chattel," she said desperately. "Would you have had me lose my identity in yours?"

Paul shrugged. "I guess not. Okay, it was as much my fault as yours. Where does that get us?"

"That's up to you," she murmured, suddenly breathless.

Paul looked down at her, his eyes dangerously compelling. They were both aware of the precipice ahead.

Suddenly the doorbell rang with an insistent peal. The moment was gone and Karen felt unutterably depressed.

Paul frowned. "Who the hell is that?" he muttered angrily.

Karen shrugged. "Perhaps it's Simon," she said thoughtfully. "It could be, you know. I'll get it."

Travers had emerged, but Paul waved him away and Karen walked swiftly to the door. She opened it wide, and immediately an onslaught of exotic perfume assailed her nostrils. She was confronted by a small, dark-haired girl dressed in a fur coat which was unmistakably mink. A hat of pink feathers adorned the girl's immaculately coiffured head, while her feet were enclosed in elegant court shoes. It was Ruth. Karen recognized her immediately and felt painfully self-conscious of her own casual attire. The clinging slacks and overblouse seemed childish and unsophisticated while Ruth appeared the epitome of femininity in her stylish clothes. Ruth's expression was one of outraged innocence, as she too recognized Karen.

Paul looked only slightly perturbed however as his fiancée advanced into the room after giving Karen a killing glance. Karen closed the door and leaned back against it feeling a surge of pride for Paul at his superb self-confidence. After all, returning home from abroad to find your fiancé's ex-wife at his apartment at this hour of the morning could only look the worst. Karen knew that were she in Ruth's position she would be fuming, as indeed Ruth was.

She had halted in the centre of the lounge and was staring angrily at Paul.

"I suppose there must be an explanation for this," she remarked coldly. "I'd be interested to hear it."

Paul shrugged his broad shoulders lightly and Ruth said: "It seems I came back at the wrong moment."

"Why should you imagine that?" Paul said, amused in spite of himself. It was rather a musical comedy situation after all. "No, Ruth, Karen's reason for being here is quite legitimate."

"I must say I'm dying to hear why," said Ruth, without much confidence.

"Things are not always what they seem," remarked Paul slowly.

Karen's eyes widened. That Paul should make such a remark when he had been so keen to believe the worst of her! After the affair with Lewis he had no room for complaint, she thought angrily.

Ruth turned and looked contemptuously at Karen, her eyes taking in the slacks and overblouse and finding them sadly wanting.

"I must say for a woman who supposedly left her husband you seem to find innumerable reasons for hanging around him," she said rudely.

Karen flushed and Paul said: "This affair has nothing to do with you, Ruth."

Karen interrupted this. "Don't bother, Paul," she said quietly. "I can fight my own battles if I have to. Your charming fiancée is simply proving what unpleasant suspicions of you she harbours. She obviously wants to believe the worst and that we have been behaving outrageously, so why should I deny it?"

Ruth's face changed from incredulous speculation to disbelief.

"I am quite willing to hear the explanation," she retorted. "You would like us to split up, wouldn't you . . . Miss Stacey . . . you made a big mistake when you allowed Paul to divorce you." She smiled disarmingly at

Paul. "Of course I believe you, darling."

Karen clasped her hands. Ruth held all the aces.

"Karen's sister is expecting a baby and has run away," said Paul quietly.

"Oh!" Ruth was silent for a moment. "Not ... Simon, surely?"

"Yes, Simon," replied Paul, frowning.

"How disgusting! She must be a ..."

"Hey, steady on," said Karen angrily. "My sister is no tramp. She thinks she's in love with Simon, fool though she is."

Ruth looked disdainful. "Couldn't you have telephoned about this, then?"

"I asked her to come," said Paul slowly.

This shocked Ruth and Karen's fingernails dug hard into her palms.

"I see." Ruth pulled off her gloves. "Well, darling, I'm home now, so we can both sort everything out together, can't we? I'm sure poor Simon must have been encouraged shamelessly –"

That was too much for Karen. No one, knowing Simon, could believe he needed encouragement. He was notoriously fickle and untrustworthy. Surely even Ruth must be aware of that. But maybe it was just another attempt on Ruth's part to annoy her. After all, she had looked at her as though she was beneath contempt when Karen opened the door in the first place. But to criticize herself and to criticize Sandra, whom she did not even know, were two entirely different things.

Recklessly, Karen retaliated: "And I suppose you imagine it runs in the family, Miss Delaney? After all, you've only been away a few days and here I am in Paul's apartment, having just breakfasted with him! Now what does that make me?"

"Paul!" exclaimed Ruth faintly, putting a hand to her throat in horror.

"Karen!" Paul's voice was appealing, but Karen was past caring what either of them thought.

"Don't worry, Paul," she snapped bitterly. "I'm not going to tell any tales out of school. Let your fiancée put her own construction on the situation, and if she comes up with the wrong solution, then hard luck, or maybe I should say it serves you right, because you were quick enough to jump to conclusions where I was concerned two years ago, weren't you?"

Paul stared at her incredulously, and Ruth seemed speechless. Karen compressed her lips. Suddenly she felt like a spoilt child trying to justify its naughtiness.

Without another word, she snatched up her coat and ran out of the apartment, slamming the door behind her. She heard Paul's grated "Karen!" but she did not stop. Instead she ran into the lift and set it in motion before he could stop her.

After Karen had gone there was an electric silence for several minutes. Every word that Karen had said was buzzing around in Paul's head, and somehow he could not rid himself of the feeling that he had been mistaken about her all along. Now, seeing Ruth again had not straightened out his tangled emotions as he had thought. Instead, he felt resentful at her untimely interruption of his conversation with his ex-wife.

Ruth eventually broke the silence, by saying: "Well, Paul, you don't seem very pleased to see me, I must say." Her tone was petulant.

Paul clenched his fists. "Oh, don't be ridiculous, Ruth," he snapped, impatiently. Then he sighed. "You're back earlier than I expected."

Ruth tossed her head. "Obviously."

Paul frowned, and Ruth, sensing she must not say too much, crossed to his side and reaching up, kissed him. "There, darling, don't worry. Ruthie trusts you!"

Paul hid a sense of distaste at her touch. "Are – are your parents with you?"

"Yes, darling." Ruth hid her annoyance. "They went to the hotel. I wanted to surprise you."

Paul shrugged his shoulders. "You certainly did that,

but anyway, did you have a good trip?"

Ruth began to tell him about their journey over and he tried to concentrate. This was Ruth, his fiancée, the girl he intended to marry. Why was the prospect of that event now so grim? Why when he wanted to be natural did he feel strung up and tense? He knew he should explain about Karen, tell Ruth that she had only been hurt and angry and that what she had said was only defiance, but the words would not come. His thoughts were still with Karen. She had looked so lost and defenceless when she left, for all her brave words. She acted so impulsively, so independently, and yet he felt sure she felt neither strong nor independent. Her words were beginning to have meaning for him. He found himself wanting to believe her in everything. This alone was enough to disturb him. If she had been telling the truth all along and Martin had been lying, then the possibilities were tremendous.

Looking at the irritated face of his fiancée, he wondered for the first time whether he could ever live seriously with another woman. Prior to Karen he had found women physically attractive but mentally boring. In his relationship with Ruth he had not explored this possibility. He had still been licking his wounds, when Ruth would came into his life and the fact that she drew him out of his inertia alone had seemed enough. Now, as he considered the facts again, he began doubting whether Ruth would provide the necessary stimulation he would need. With Karen their marriage had been nothing if not stimulating. Karen. Karen. Karen. His mind buzzing with the thoughts of her and he despaired of ever getting her out of his system. Perhaps if she had never come back into his life he would have peacefully married Ruth without all this soul-searching, but now it seemed he couldn't entertain the idea.

And if, after all this, he did marry Ruth, would he find their marriage empty and turn to another woman like Simon had done? Perhaps if Simon had had a wife like

Karen this whole affair might never have happened.

He was appalled by the turn his mind was taking. Karen had generated all this, this resentment of his chosen environment and his chosen wife. Karen, who had been so much more than a housewife; and who had left him a shattered man. A man who now was willing to believe anything to exonerate her from the blame of their separation!

He became aware that Ruth was staring at him in annoyance, for he seemed to have drifted miles away from her. And she could tell by his expression that he had not listened to a word she had said.

"What on earth are you thinking about, honey?" she queried, trying to behave calmly when anger was tearing her apart. How dared he behave so tardily with her? It had all begun since he began seeing Karen Stacey again, and her anger towards the other girl knew no bounds.

Paul gathered his thoughts. "I'm sorry, Ruth," he said, raking a hand through his hair. "What were you saying?"

Ruth calmed down. "I asked what you intend to do about Sandra."

Paul frowned. In his own tortuous thoughts he had almost forgotten the problems of Sandra and Simon.

"Oh, yes," he murmured now, frowning. "Excuse me for a moment, Ruth. I have a telephone call to make."

Lewis Martin sat moodily in his office staring at the design on the desk before him without interest. Work had become an anathema to him of late, and he was obsessed with thoughts of Karen . . . and Paul Frazer.

When he had assisted Karen to obtain her divorce it had been for purely personal motives. He admired her tremendously and although their relationship had remained on a business footing he was convinced it was only a matter of time before she realized he would make her a good husband.

His first marriage had not been a success. His wife had

been a cold, unfeeling woman and her death had been a relief rather than a tragedy to him. Then meeting the warm and lively Karen he had been immediately attracted and determined to have her.

The last few weeks had therefore been a torment to him. Knowing she was meeting Paul Frazer again had tortured his disturbed emotions and he found himself degenerating into a moody recluse.

Karen herself had not helped by her easy references to Paul, and to find him visiting the flat, the flat which he, Lewis, had bought for her, had incensed him. Without really thinking that he had no claims on Karen, he began considering her attitude towards him as one of betrayal, and he felt more like a cheated husband than anything else. He did not stop to think how strange such an attitude might seem, but he had been aware of late of Karen's changed attitude towards him. No longer did she come to him for advice and she no longer invited him to the flat as she had frequently done in the past. He was jealous, painfully and violently jealous, and Karen was either deliberately flaunting herself or was completely unaware of his feelings. He had already decided it was the former in his contorted mind.

When the telephone rang he lifted the receiver with alacrity. It might be Karen!

"Is that Mr. Lewis Martin?" asked a woman's voice, with a strong southern American accent.

Lewis frowned. "Yes," he replied. "Can I help you?"

"We can maybe help each other, honey," replied the voice sweetly. "I'm Ruth Delaney. Need I say more?"

Lewis's fingers tightened on the telephone.

"No," he muttered. "What do you want?"

"Well now, I have some information that might not please you. Paul broke off his engagement to me today. Are you interested?"

Lewis felt his heart begin to pound heavily in his ears. Paul Frazer had broken his engagement. There could be only one reason for that!

"I'm very interested, Miss Delaney," he said, his voice thickening. "Could we meet for lunch, say?"

"If you like," she replied swiftly. "Where?"

Lewis named a restaurant and a time and then rang off. He understood clearly why Ruth Delaney had chosen to ring him. She had a stake in this herself. She wanted Paul Frazer and she also knew that he had been the co-respondent in the divorce case. What greater reason had he for wanting to marry Karen? They were in similar positions and could perhaps help each other.

And yet, he thought dully, if Karen did not want him, what more could he do? His hands were clammy with sweat and he realized he was running a temperature. His feelings towards Karen were like a fire burning in his veins and soon it felt as though it would consume him. There had got to be a showdown. He could not go on like this indefinitely.

He thrust himself out of his chair and walked across to his window. Looking down on the street below he felt a strong desire to push open the window and jump. Clenching his fists he turned away. What madness was this that caused him to feel this way? Why couldn't his life have gone along in the same old way with Karen coming into the office regularly and he always knowing he could contact her when he wanted to?

It was all a racing game with time and he was not sure he wanted to play it any longer.

He lit a cigarette with shaking fingers. He had never dreamed he could feel this way about any woman, and now that he did it nauseated him. He must see this Ruth woman at lunch time and make her understand his position too. She must be made to see that he wanted Karen at any price and then . . . later . . . he must see Karen herself . . . before it was too late.

CHAPTER SEVEN

PAUL rang Karen at twelve o'clock. She was trying unsuccessfully to read a woman's magazine in the sitting-room at her mother's home when the telephone pealed.

Beating her mother to the hall, Karen lifted the receiver.

"Yes?" she said, her voice toneless.

"Sandra is in Brighton," said Paul's voice. "Simon gave me the address. He's in quite a state, as you can imagine. He didn't know himself until this morning. He got a nice little letter in the post explaining everything. He came to the apartment in a flat spin. I really believe he had given up all hopes of ever seeing her again. He doesn't seem to have any emotional leanings in that direction at the moment."

"Oh!" Karen sighed heavily. She mouthed the gist of the conversation to her mother who was leaning against the banister rail. She immediately burst into tears of relief and Karen said:

"Thanks for everything, Paul."

"Yes, well, Karen, I've had a word with Aaron Bernard. He wants to come..."

"Oh, not now..." she began achingly, her pulses beginning to act in that disturbed manner.

"Yes, now," retorted Paul quietly. "He wants to come around earlier than we expected, at about two o'clock, and then after he has gone I'll run you and your mother down to Brighton to bring Sandra back."

Karen was astounded. She had expected to have to drive down to Brighton herself to bring Sandra back.

"But... but what about Ruth?" she exclaimed, remembering her rude treatment of the girl earlier in the day.

"I'll handle Ruth," replied Paul softly. "Does that suit you?"

"Of course it suits me," exclaimed Karen exasperatedly. "How could it be otherwise? When will I see you then?"

"I'll come with Aaron," he answered. "See you," and he rang off.

Karen replaced the receiver, bewildered. He had not sounded angry as she had expected and she could not understand it. He had sounded angry when she left the apartment this morning. Probably he and Ruth had talked it all over and she was amused by it all. Perhaps she would drive down to Brighton with them. After all, the Facel Vega was certainly big enough.

Her mother was wiping her eyes, and Karen outlined how Paul had found out.

"Sandra will have to go away and have the baby," went on Karen. "You wouldn't want her to stay here, would you, Mother?"

"Go away? Oh, yes, I suppose so. I suppose you and I will have to go and get her."

"Paul is driving us down," said Karen with a shrug. "He suggested it."

"Oh, thank goodness. I had visions of us having a scene with Sandra and her refusing to come. With Paul that won't happen. He's more likely to carry her out bodily if she makes any fuss."

"She won't fuss Paul," said Karen with definition. "He can handle Sandra. We both know that."

"Yes. It's a pity really. My first grandchild, too. You never gave me any, Karen." Her voice was reproachful.

"No," said Karen shortly. "Gosh, no wonder Sandra lives in a make-believe world! Here you are romancing about a baby that was causing you to have hysterics six hours ago."

"You've never understood me," said Madeline, softly and tearfully. "No wonder you didn't make a success of marriage. You expect too much of people."

Karen ignored this. Her mother was taking out her pique on her, that Sandra had failed to confide in her about the baby.

"Well, I'll go," said Karen abruptly. She pulled on her coat. "We'll pick you up at about three o'clock, right?"

"All right, dear. Thank you for all you've done."

"Don't mention it," said Karen dryly, and opened the front door. She did not want gratitude. She felt insincere and insecure. No longer was her little world a safe place. Fate had taken a hand and made a mockery of her life. Or was that fair? Had she not ruined her own life years ago? What price now a job and a life of her own?

Karen made herself a snack in lieu of lunch and then dressed in a slim-fitting suit of tangerine wool. She looked tall and slim and lovely, and was glad. She wanted to look lovely for Paul, even if Ruth was to be there.

When the telephone rang she thought it would be Paul and said:

"Karen here. Is anything wrong?"

"Wrong? No. Why should there be anything wrong?" asked Lewis's voice shortly. "So you're home at last. I've been trying to get you for half an hour."

"I've been in the bath," she replied. "I probably didn't hear the telephone." She resented anew his proprietorial tone. "I was out this morning because there has been some more trouble over Sandra."

"Indeed?" Lewis sounded adequately surprised. "And I suppose you had to contact Frazer again?"

"Why, yes. How did you know?"

"I didn't. I merely put two and two together and made four."

Karen frowned. "Oh, I see. Why are you ringing, Lewis?"

"I would like to see you," he replied smoothly. "Soon."

Karen shrugged her slim shoulders. "What do you want to see me about?"

"Why . . . er . . . the new designs. What else?" he asked innocently.

Karen bit her lip. There it was again. That certain

something about Lewis's manner which she could not put her finger on. She frowned. What could she say? He was her employer after all. She had no desire to see him, but what could she do? Perhaps it was time to tell him she was terminating her employment. She could say she had got another job, even if she had not. He would be none the wiser.

"Will tomorrow do?" she asked, realizing how full today was going to be.

"Why not tonight? Have you got an engagement?"

Not at the moment, she thought wildly. Would it not be as well to see him and get it over with once and for all?

"All right," she agreed reluctantly. "Will you come here?"

"No. I want you to come to the office," he said firmly. "I have to work late in any case and I can best explain my plans here."

Karen hesitated. At least seeing him in the office would keep everything on a businesslike basis.

"Very well. What time?"

"Seven will be fine," he said. "Does that suit you?"

Karen mentally calculated how long it would take them to go to Brighton and come back. Seven might be a little early.

"Make it half-past," she said.

"All right, Karen. Good-bye for the present."

He rang off and Karen replaced her receiver. She stood staring at the telephone, wishing he had not rung today of all days. A shiver slithered down her spine. Lewis had sounded so strange, so cold and yet pressing. She sighed. Goodness, what imagination could do to a person!

She checked her hair in the mirror as there was a knock at the door. Shaking off her apprehension, she went to open it. Paul was there and with him was the middle-aged man with receding grey hair that she recognized as Aaron Bernard.

Paul smiled as they came in and introduced his companion. Aaron Bernard smiled rather absently at her, his eyes already wandering around the room, seeking the paintings he had come to see.

"You look around at your leisure, Aaron," said Paul, patting the older man on the back. "I want a word with Karen."

"Good enough," agreed Aaron, nodding at Karen who was led by Paul out of the lounge and into the minute kitchen.

"Did you tell your mother everything?" he asked when they were alone in the kitchen.

"Yes," she nodded. "Where is she staying?" She smiled. "Sandra, I mean."

"It's a small country pub just outside Brighton, Simon says they've been there for drinks in the past, and Sandra always liked it."

"I see. Good for Sandra!" she said wryly.

"Are you nervous?" he asked lazily. "About Aaron, I mean."

His words were so like hers that she was sure he was mocking her.

"Naturally," she cried restlessly. "I want to know his decision, and yet I'm afraid to hear it."

"So. I brought you out here so that you wouldn't be breathing down his neck while he studied the pictures."

"As if I would!" she exclaimed indignantly.

"Nevertheless, you admit you want to know his decision. Of course you do. And if my opinion is of any consequence, I think you're going to be a success. Doesn't that enthral you; excite you?"

Karen sighed. In truth her feelings about her paintings had faded into insignificance compared to her dealings with Paul and although she was pleased that a man of Aaron Bernard's character considered them worth looking at she found the initial thrill had palled. Her work was no longer of supreme importance to her. She had grown out of that stage.

To Paul, however, she said: "Of course it excites me. I feel quite exhilarated. The only thing that mars my pleasure is the worry over Sandra."

Paul lit a cigarette. "I shouldn't place too much emphasis on that young woman," he murmured. "It may turn out to be a storm in a teacup."

Karen looked sceptical. That did not seem very likely to her.

"Relax!" he exclaimed in an amused tone. Then he turned and pushed open the door leading into the lounge. He walked through into the room and Karen, left alone, leaned over the sink feeling physically sick. What was Paul playing at? He had not mentioned this morning's fiasco as she had expected, nor had he mentioned Ruth.

Remembering Lewis's weird telephone call and now Paul's indifference, it seemed that the whole world was going slightly off key. Or was it she who was providing all these riddles? Could it be that she was so emotionally disturbed that she was dreaming things that did not really happen? She laughed without humour. Things were what you made them, and she was allowing the trouble over Sandra and her subsequent longing for Paul to get her down.

She rubbed her heaving stomach, calmed herself and walked casually into the lounge. Aaron Bernard and Paul were talking together and looked speculatively at her as she entered.

"Well, gentlemen?" she said, forcing a bantering tone. "Have you reached your verdict?"

Aaron Bernard smiled encouragingly.

"We have indeed," he said, looking round at the abstracts. "I'm happy to say that I like them and that I'm very pleased Paul saw fit to tell me about them. Some of them are naturally not as good as others, but in the main the overall feeling is excellent. I think if you go on in this manner you will certainly become an excellent impressionist. If you can produce some more by the autumn I'll certainly consider giving you a one-man show at my gallery in October."

Karen's face went pale and she sank down on to a chair, her hands pressed to her cheeks.

"You . . . you wouldn't fool me about this, Paul?" she gasped, her mind chaotic.

Paul shook his head blithely and Aaron Bernard smiled indulgently. Seeing her rather strained expression, Paul crossed to the drinks and poured her a stiff whisky. He put it in her hand and made her sip it at once.

"No," said Aaron finally. "I am most pleased to have a first opportunity of seeing these pictures. How long have you been painting?"

"About two years now," replied Karen weakly, looking up at Paul. Those two years which had been so long in retrospect.

"Then it's amazing," said Aaron with a shrug. "If my opinion proves correct, in a couple of years you will find you need no further occupation. That is if you wish to give up the work you are doing at present. I understand you are a commercial designer."

Karen nodded helplessly. "I can't take it in. It's so wonderful."

"Then come and see me next week," said Aaron, smiling understandingly. "When you have had time to collect your thoughts you will find the proposition is quite a good one. Would next Wednesday suit you? Twelve o'clock at the gallery. We could perhaps lunch together."

"That would be marvellous," agreed Karen earnestly. "I don't know how to express my thanks, Mr. Bernard."

He shrugged. "You could begin by offering me a drink," he remarked, smiling, and Karen blushed and rose to her feet.

"Of course. How remiss of me. What will you have? And you, Paul?"

After they had accepted their drinks, Aaron said:

"I am a business man, Miss Stacey, whatever else I may be. I think your paintings constitute good business.

At the moment the market is booming."

They chatted together for a while about painting and painters in general, and then Aaron excused himself and left, reminding Karen of their proposed meeting the following week. After he had gone, Karen turned to Paul:

"He's a very nice man, isn't he?" She smiled. "Thank you."

Paul shrugged. "Well, well," he mused. "Karen Stacey, artist."

Karen hesitated for a moment and then she ran across to him and flung herself into his arms, tears scalding her cheeks.

"Oh, Paul!" she breathed achingly. "What can I say . . . or do?"

"Just be a success," said Paul rather abruptly, and gently disengaged himself. He didn't want Karen's gratitude.

Karen, not understanding, felt the cold fingers of loneliness touch her heart again, and without a word she lifted her mohair coat and put it on, ignoring his attempt to assist her.

"Come on," she murmured, wiping the back of her hand across her eyes. "I expect Mother will be waiting impatiently for us."

The journey to her mother's was accomplished in silence and Madeline was ready on the step, waiting for them. Her eyes widened appreciatively as she slid into the luxurious automobile. This was her idea of living. Luxury had always appealed to Madeline Stacey.

Paul assisted her and then slid back in beside Karen. His thigh brushed against hers and Karen felt something like an electric shock at the touch of his body. She was so overwhelmingly conscious of the nearness of him that it was like a physical pain. His eyes looked into hers for a moment, probingly, and she felt her heart flutter and subside again as he turned on the ignition.

Her mother spoke and broke the tension.

"Which hotel is Sandra staying at?" she asked, addressing her remarks to them both.

Paul expertly passed a stationary vehicle and then said:

"The Barn Owl." He smiled dryly. "It's hardly a hotel. More of a public house."

"Oh, Paul!" exclaimed Madeline. "Sandra! Staying at a place like that. Is it in Brighton?"

"No, just outside. A village called Barneton, I believe. Simon gave me directions. It's apparently clean, and quite good," he went on, glancing at Karen. "Simon has often taken his girl-friends there for drinks."

"And the rest," cried Madeline achingly. "Really, Paul, how can Simon act so rashly? And he a married man, too."

"Don't ask me," answered Paul coolly. "I'm not his keeper, any more than you are Sandra's."

Madeline looked hurt, and Karen reached for her cigarettes. She lit two and handed one to Paul. He took his naturally as though they had always done this. It had been a favourite habit in the old days, but no longer.

The journey to Barneton was accomplished in an hour and Paul drove through the village to the Barn Owl.

It turned out to be a rather olde worlde public house with black beams and brick fireplaces. Karen quite liked the look of it and said so. Paul turned the car into the small car park. The Facel Vega dwarfed the rather limited parking space.

Paul slid out, followed by Karen, and while he helped Madeline out, Karen pulled on her coat. Paul too, put on the thick duffel-coat lying on the back seat, for the scent of the sea was unmistakable and the wind blowing offshore was cold and damp.

They walked through a low door into the building. Paul had to bend his head and even Karen felt she only just made it under the beam. It was not yet opening time and the place looked deserted. An elderly woman appeared from behind the reception desk and approached them stiffly.

"Yes, can I help you?" she said, taking in their appearance at a glance. She obviously recognized the cut of Paul's clothes for an ingratiating smile came to her thin lips and she waited patiently for his reply.

"We're looking for a Miss Sandra Stacey," replied Paul smoothly. "I understand she is staying here."

The woman looked surprised. "There's no one of that name here," she denied politely. "I'm afraid you've come to the wrong place."

Paul was unperturbed. "Then did a young girl register here either late last night or early this morning?"

The woman's eyes narrowed. "Well . . . I . . . yes, a Miss Nicholson she said her name was."

Madeline gasped audibly and the woman said suspiciously:

"Is she in trouble? Or are you friends of hers?"

"She's in no trouble," replied Paul. "This is her mother and sister. She ran away from home yesterday, and we have come to find her."

"Oh." The woman relaxed. "I see."

"And is she in? asked Madeline impatiently. "I must see her."

"Yes. She's in her room," said the woman slowly. "I'll go and tell her you're here."

"Don't bother," said Paul shortly. "If you tell her mother which room is hers, I think she would like to see her alone for a minute."

The woman frowned but shrugged. "Very well. Do I understand that Miss Nicholson will be checking out again today?"

Paul bit his lip. "I expect so, why?"

"Well, it's been very inconvenient for me," she said irritatedly. "I've had to put clean sheets on that bed and make special meals . . ."

Paul looked cynical. "I think we can settle that," he murmured with an understanding smile, and the woman smiled in return.

It was blackmail, thought Karen, sickened by her mother's total disregard for this angle. She was too eager to find Sandra and no doubt tell her how foolish she had been but that she forgave her.

The woman showed Madeline which room to go to and then she and Paul disappeared into the office behind the reception desk, while Karen wandered aimlessly into the lounge. It was quite a pleasant room, with small tables and a long, low bar, quite out of character to the rest of the building.

She was not there alone long before Paul joined her, putting his wallet back into his pocket. She flushed, feeling unreasonably guilty.

"This is quite a nice place," she said, forcing herself to speak lightly.

"I shall like it better when we're leaving it behind," he replied harshly. "We're going straight back to London and to a doctor I know."

"A doctor? For Sandra?" Karen looked surprised.

"Of course. I want this myth solving one way or the other. I personally don't believe that so convenient a thing as a baby could happen. It might be true, of course, and by seeing a doctor we can confirm it, right?"

Karen clasped her hands together.

"Oh, Paul, I really hope she has been making it up, even though it's a cruel and horrible thing to do. What a relief it would be!"

"I know," Paul smiled at her suddenly, his eyes warm and gentle. "And I personally will have something to say to our Miss Sandra if it *is* all lies. Poor old Simon! I really felt sorry for him this morning."

Karen shivered and wrapped her coat round her warmly. The room was unheated and cold and she felt frozen. Paul in his thick coat and dark suit looked strong and vital and she felt utterly weak and defenceless. If only she dared tell him how she was feeling. What would he say? Would he remind her of his other obligations and of the fast approaching date of his marriage?

"Tell me," she said suddenly. "Did you have lunch with Ruth?"

Paul shook his head. "As far as I know, Ruth had lunch with her parents. Why?"

"I just wondered whether she objected to your coming down here this afternoon."

Paul looked thoughtfully at her.

"No, she did not object," he remarked smoothly. "What Ruth thinks now is of no consequence to me."

"No consequence . . ." echoed Karen wildly, unable to prevent the sudden leaping of her heart.

Paul looked down at her and she felt her face burning at the expression in his eyes. What did it mean? What did it all mean?

And then before any more could be said there were footsteps in the hall and Sandra came stalking angrily into the lounge, followed by a tearful Madeline. She looked utterly dejected and defiantly youthful.

"Well, well. Hello, Sandra," said Paul, reluctantly moving away from Karen. "What a pleasant surprise!"

Sandra flushed scarlet. "Don't make me laugh," she said coldly. "What is this? The Sunday school outing?"

"No. The posse," replied Paul, a smile playing round his mouth. "Aren't you pleased to see us, honey?"

"You don't need me to answer that," said Sandra bitterly.

"True enough," said Paul, the smile leaving his face. "Do you know what a menace you are, young woman? Come on. Outside. Where's your suitcase?"

"It's in the hall," said Madeline weakly. "Have you paid the bill . . . if there was one?"

"I've given her freedom to go if that's what you mean," nodded Paul. "Come on. Let's get out of here."

The car was deliciously warm after the lukewarm hotel and even Sandra found the luxurious comfort enjoyable after her poky little room and hard-sprung bed.

Paul drove out of the car park and then trod on the accelerator and sent the car surging forward.

Then he said bluntly: "So you're expecting a baby, Sandra?"

Sandra was obviously not expecting such a frontal attack and looked mildly uncomfortable.

"In November," she said defiantly.

"Quite a long way off," he remarked dryly. "Are you quite sure?"

Karen bit her lip and glanced back at her sister's scarlet face.

"Of course I am sure," replied Sandra coldly. "Women have ways of knowing these things, you know. I'm not a child."

"I'm sure you're not," agreed Paul smoothly. "A child wouldn't have thought out this complicated plan. Just out of interest, how did you get here, anyway?"

"I came down last night. I hitched a lift in a lorry."

"You did what!" exclaimed Madeline. "Good lord, Sandra, you might have been raped or murdered. You foolhardy infant!"

"I am not an infant," gasped Sandra churlishly. "You don't understand at all, none of you."

"No, and nor do you," replied Paul easily. "You're in a pretty desperate situation, young Sandra."

"How do you make that out? I love Simon. What would be simpler?"

"It would be simpler if Simon loved you," replied Paul cruelly. "Would you care to hear what he said this morning when he told me your address?"

"He told you my address?" she gasped. "Oh, how could he?"

"How do you think we found you?" exclaimed Karen impatiently.

"I suppose so," said Sandra dully. "All right," Paul, what did he say?"

"He begged me to come down here today and tell you that he was through. Why else do you think I'm here? Don't you think he would have come to find you himself if he really loved you?"

Sandra was looking a little less sure of herself.

"He's going to get a divorce," she cried shrilly.

"I think not," said Paul coldly. "One has to be cruel to be kind, Sandra. Poor Simon has no intention of marrying you. Could you imagine him saddled with a wife and child without a job? I certainly won't help him."

Sandra burst into tears. "Some brother, you are!" she cried bitterly.

Paul shrugged. "Whatever I may be is beside the point. I honestly tell you, Sandra, Simon doesn't want to marry you. He enjoyed your company, but he usually loves a girl and then leaves her. You must have known his reputation. You have only yourself to blame."

"But the baby!" she cried pitifully. "It's Simon's baby. He's got to marry me."

"Is that why you made it up?" asked Paul bluntly. "To force Simon's hand?"

"Made it up?" Sandra was shocked into speechlessness.

Paul shrugged, and Karen wondered if he had gone too far. Sandra was very pale and wan, and she began believing that she really was pregnant.

"Karen!" wailed Sandra at last. "Are you going to let him speak to me like that? Your own sister?"

Karen bit her lip and glanced sideways at Paul. Paul's eyes were dark and enigmatic.

"Leave Karen out of this!" he muttered. "It has nothing to do with her. You got yourself into this and you alone can get yourself out."

"And you don't believe me!" exclaimed Sandra. "Paul, I always liked you, I even thought I was in love with you once. How can you be so cruel!"

"Sandra! You've said you're not a child. Very well then, you must be treated as an adult. And as an adult I don't think you are expecting a baby. In fact, I'd go so far as to bet on it."

Madeline began to cry. It had been too much for her

and Karen felt a ridiculous desire to laugh. What a strange bunch they were, the Stacey family. Little wonder if Paul found little to appeal to him in herself.

"Well, I am," insisted Sandra at last. "I really am."

"Then we'll go directly to my own doctor and confirm it," said Paul abruptly. Karen thought he looked rather disgusted now and she wondered seriously whether Sandra could be lying.

"A doctor?" It was obvious from Sandra's face that she had not considered this contingency. "I don't need to see a doctor for ages yet."

"Maybe not, but I want this settled once and for all. If you're telling the truth you have nothing to be afraid of."

Sandra burst into violent sobbing. "You're against me! You're all against me. Even Simon is against me, going away to Nottingham and never even bothering to write. I had to do something ..." Her voice trailed away.

Karen felt sick. It was pretty obvious now that Sandra had indeed been lying all the time. Madeline was speechless for a moment and then she said:

"You bad, wicked girl! How dare you act like this! It nearly killed me, do you realize that?"

"I love Simon, I love him, I love him!" cried Sandra, ignoring her mother. "Doesn't anybody care?"

"We all care what happens to you," said Paul surprisingly. "Be thankful you really are all right. It could so easily have been true, couldn't it?"

"Yes. Simon knows that. That's why ..."

"That's why he was so panic-stricken," finished Paul grimly. "All right, Sandra. You can calm down now."

He was unutterably relieved. For a moment there he had wondered if his hunch had been wrong. If it had he would have regretted his harsh words although they were all true.

"You can't get everything you want, simply by deceit and lies," said Karen angrily. "Sandra, you sicken me, you really do! Have you no decent feelings for anyone but yourself?"

Sandra did not reply and Karen lit two cigarettes, and after handing one to Paul she drew on hers thankfully. The crisis was past and now she felt dreadfully aware of the anti-climax.

Sandra cried the rest of the way home. Her face was blotched and her eyes were puffy, but she was still as defiant as ever.

Once at her mother's house, they all went inside. Liza was waiting for them, but withdrew when she saw Sandra's swollen features. Now was not the time for platitudes. Sandra flung her coat on to a chair in the hall and would have gone upstairs, but Paul caught her arm, his face grim.

"I want a word with you, young woman," he said firmly, "come on, in here."

He manoeuvred her into the sitting-room, closing the door firmly behind them, leaving Madeline and Karen in the hall. Madeline frowned and would have opened the door, but Karen shook her head, stopping her. Whatever Paul had to say to Sandra would be better said in private.

In the sitting-room Sandra faced Paul with only a little of her former defiance. Her ruse to claim Simon utterly had failed miserably and she felt unaccountably relieved for some reason now that it was over. She had known all along, of course, that she was wrong, but that had not helped. If only her mother had not created such a cotton wool world around her she might have grown up more like Karen and thus would not have felt the need to break out and shock everybody. She supposed it was basically a sense of insecurity founded on her mother's rather weak attempts at motherhood.

She listened to Paul's steadfast voice explaining how she had hurt her mother and caused anxiety to them all. He barely mentioned Simon, and she supposed he thought that Simon deserved the hours of purgatory he had spent. He was probably right. At the moment Simon seemed very different from the gay companion she had known and believed she had loved.

Afterwards he let her go and she went upstairs to repair her make-up and make herself presentable. Paul met Karen in the hall.

She smiled. "Thanks, for everything," she murmured.

"Don't thank me," he said softly. "Now, are you coming with me?"

Karen hesitated. "Mother is still very upset," she began.

"All right," Paul nodded. "How about later, then? We could have dinner."

Karen clasped her hands together. "I have to see Lewis at half-past seven, I'm afraid."

Paul's expression hardened. "Indeed?" he muttered. "That's that, then."

Karen shrugged helplessly. "I'm sorry, Paul. But I never thought . . ."

"Don't worry," he said coldly. "It wasn't important."

Karen felt cold inside. "I have to go to the office," she explained awkwardly. "But I don't expect I shall be long."

Paul hesitated. He wanted to believe her.

"All right," he murmured, his eyes softening. "How about coming to the apartment after you leave Martin? We could have dinner there, if you like."

It couldn't be true! Paul was actually asking her to go to his apartment!

"That would be wonderful," she whispered. Ruth could not possibly be bothering him now. But why? The prospect was breathtaking.

"Good." He bent his head swiftly and kissed her mouth, and then he was gone.

Karen stood immobile. Could this be really true? Surely it was not a dream after all this time. She wanted it to be true. Oh, how she wanted it to be true.

Things were at last beginning to make sense. Sandra was home and was no longer in any danger from Simon. In addition, if Karen should go back to Paul she would have the guiding hand from him that she so badly needed. Madeline would be pleased, of course for more mercenary reasons, but for Karen it was Paul himself that she wanted, now and always.

She left her mother after having tea and sandwiches with her. Sandra had emerged from her room looking suitably chastened, and although Karen doubted whether Paul's lecture would have any long-lasting effects she was undoubtedly prepared to be more amiable.

Karen walked back to her flat, enjoying the feel of the cool night air on her face. It was a clear, starlit evening and she felt the old excitement welling up in her. To-night she was to see Paul again and for no other reason than that he had asked her to. There would be no discussions about Sandra or Simon or Ruth. Only themselves and nothing else.

She dressed in a dark red velvet dress and wore her loose mohair coat. She looked bright-eyed and sparkling but could not help it. She was happy! Happy as she had not been for years.

The offices of Lewis Martin Textiles were in darkness apart from the one light at the top of the building where Lewis had his office. Karen felt her pleasure wilt slightly as she entered the building, and tentative fingers of apprehension probed her mind. Shrugging off the feeling, she took the lift up to his office. She knocked and entered to find Lewis sitting at his desk, doodling on a pad with a ball-point pen.

She thought he looked edgy and tired and his usually well-dressed appearance was marred by the looseness of his collar and the ruffled untidiness of his hair. He seemed to have been running his hands through it often, and Karen wondered what was troubling him. He was definitely a disturbed man, and she felt rather uncomfortable in his presence.

At her entrance he rose to his feet, his eyes sweeping her appearance with studied intensity.

"Ah, Karen," he murmured, a smile coming to his lips. "Won't you sit down?"

Karen subsided on to the low chair opposite him and looked expectantly at him. Lewis seated himself also and watched her as she lit a cigarette. To her annoyance her fingers were trembling, and Lewis noticed this.

"Are you cold, Karen?" he asked.

"No." She repudiated the suggestion with a forced smile.

"Nervous, then?" he murmured, his smile mocking.

"Why should I be nervous of you, Lewis?" she asked, determined to retain a lightness in her manner.

He shrugged. "Why, indeed? You know I only have your welfare at heart, don't you, Karen? I've always been a good friend to you, haven't I?"

Karen bit her lip. What was he leading up to?

"Yes, Lewis," she murmured in reply. "I think so."

"You think so," he echoed. "What do you mean by that remark?" His eyes narrowed and Karen wished she had not said just those words. Truthfully, she would like to have cleared up the business of Lewis informing Paul that they were lovers, for there must be an explanation for that, but she decided that this was not the time nor the place. It was too delicate a matter. "Don't read anything into my remarks, Lewis," she said. "It was a completely innocent statement."

Lewis hesitated a moment and then nodded and rose to his feet. He had lit a cigarette and drew hard on it.

"I'm very glad you came, Karen," he said.

"Well ... shall we get on, then?" she asked a little nervously.

Lewis ran a hand through his hair again. "All in good time, Karen," he said. "I really wanted to talk to you, you know. I get so little chance these days. You're always so busy."

Karen frowned. "Hardly that, Lewis. I've been helping to keep Sandra from breaking her heart over Simon Frazer, if that's what you mean. I'm sorry if you think

I've been neglecting my work."

"You mentioned work, I didn't," he murmured with a cold smile. "We used to be such close associates, Karen. Lately you haven't seemed to want to see me at all. You rarely come in to the office."

Karen shrugged and felt herself going red.

"That's not true, Lewis," she protested. "We were never very close. You always knew we would never be more than friends."

"Friends? Ah, yes, friends. And is Paul Frazer a friend of yours now?" Lewis's eyes glittered strangely.

"Paul and I? Well, that's our affair, surely?" she replied, resenting his manner and yet somehow afraid to openly antagonize him in this mood.

"You've been seeing a lot of him lately," said Lewis in a monotone.

"And I've just told you why," she exclaimed hastily.

Lewis frowned. "And I suppose you now know he's broken his engagement to Ruth Delaney?"

There it was at last. Paul was free. It was true! Really true! She tried to contain her excitement, but it must have shown in her face for he looked piercingly at her, his eyes burning.

"No," she said at last, "I didn't know that. How did you find out?"

"I had lunch with Ruth today."

Karen was astounded. "You had lunch with Ruth? But Ruth doesn't know you."

"No, I agree. Before today we were strangers, but she rang me up because she knows how I feel about you and consequently she thought we might be able to help each other. You see, she still wants Paul Frazer just as much as I want you."

Karen blinked her eyes rapidly. This conversation was fast becoming too personal. Was this what she had been unconsciously afraid of? Lewis's growing obsession with herself and the showdown which had been inevitable? He was obviously strung up and the passionate absorption which he had always shown for his work all seemed to have been turned on her.

"Lewis!" she exclaimed. "You know that whatever happens I couldn't marry you."

"I disagree." His face was grim. "Until Frazer came back into your life you were drifting into a relationship with me that would have eventually led to marriage."

"No!" The word was torn from her. "I couldn't marry you, Lewis. Ever. I think I ought to tell you now. I'm resigning from the company. We can't go on in this way any longer."

"I agree," he muttered, his voice harsh. "That's why I asked you here this evening. But don't think you can just cast me aside like an old shoe. I've done everything for you, Karen, found you a home, employed you, most of all loved you . . ."

Karen felt awful. His degeneration shocked her, arousing her pity.

"Oh, Lewis!" she exclaimed. "I'm so sorry. Truly I am, but we were never meant to be married, you and I. You're not like me and I'm sure I'm not your type."

Lewis was going red in the face and she cried anxiously:

"Are you all right?"

"All right?" he echoed angrily. "How can I feel all right when I watch you ruining your life for a second time?"

Karen frowned. "I'm not ruining my life, Lewis."

"You're considering going back to Frazer, aren't you?" he sneered bitterly. "I thought you had more self-respect, Karen! Can't you see he's only leading you on to spurn you, once again?"

"Then why has he broken his engagement to Ruth?" she exclaimed, aware that Lewis's words still had the power to disturb her.

Lewis shrugged. "How should I know? Maybe he tired of her, too."

Karen bent her head. There was still an element of

logic in Lewis's words. Why should she imagine that Paul's interest in her was any more than a physical attraction? Hadn't he himself said almost the same thing that day at Trevayne?

She looked up. "Whatever I decide to do, Lewis, it's no concern of yours," she said clearly. "And I won't change my mind so far as you are concerned! It's no good, Lewis. You're too old for me!"

Lewis's face contorted at her words. "I wasn't too old for you when it came to citing me as co-respondent in your divorce suit!" he said violently. "You used me, Karen, and you can't deny it!"

Karen shook her head unhappily. "Oh, Lewis, you wouldn't let me fight the case. You know we were innocent. You know we could have proved it."

"How, answer me that!"

Karen got unsteadily to her feet. "No, you answer me something," she retorted, gathering confidence from indignation. "How was it that a witness should certify that we spent that particular night in the flat together? It was only one night, so why were we found out?"

Lewis bent his head, avoiding her eyes. "Obviously Paul was already seeking a divorce. He had detectives –"

"Well, how jolly convenient!" cried Karen hotly, "that's all I can say. If I didn't know you better, I'd half-believe you planned the whole thing!"

"Karen!" He was staring at her with horrified eyes. "How can you insinuate such a thing? I – who have always had your well-being at heart."

"Well, maybe I can do without your help," she said, fingering a heavy paperweight that was lying at her side of the desk.

"Can't you see," he exclaimed, shaking his head, "that I only want to support you and can care for you, be the person you can turn to in times of trouble?" He came round the desk to her side. "Karen, be reasonable! You know I'm the only person who loves you to distraction."

Karen stepped away from him. "I really think I ought

to be going, Lewis," she said uncomfortably. "Obviously, you're in no mood to talk about work, and I'm in no mood for anything else."

Lewis halted, his eyes glittering with his anger. "Don't despise me so much, Karen," he muttered. "One day you may wish you'd listened to me!"

"Are you threatening me, Lewis?"

"No, not threatening, Karen, only advising. *Paul Frazer!*" His voice grated over the words. "That man has been the bane of my life!"

Karen looked at him squarely. "You must know, Lewis, that I love Paul. I always have and I guess I always will. Oh, for a time you convinced me I was being foolish, and I began to think I was fooling myself, but it's no good, I see that now. I'm sorry if I've hurt you, Lewis, but there's nothing I can do."

Lewis caught her shoulders when she would have moved away, and thrust his face close to hers. "Once before Frazer thought you were my mistress," he said harshly. "But either he's accepted that it was a fleeting thing on your part or else you've told him the truth and he's chosen to believe you. I wonder what his reaction would be, however, if he found that you were my mistress – now."

Karen stared at him incredulously. "What do you mean?" she asked breathlessly, hardly daring to consider what he was suggesting.

Lewis's eyebrows raised. "Surely you know what I mean," he taunted her. "This office building is deserted, and we're alone. What's to prevent me from making love to you? Or should I say *who?*"

Karen was horrified. "You're crazy!" she exclaimed, glancing towards the door involuntarily, wondering if he was really serious.

Lewis shrugged. "Am I? Why do you say that? You're a beautiful woman, Karen, the only woman I've ever really loved. Why should you imagine I would hesitate to take every chance to make you mine – to rid myself of annoying competition? Because of a surety, Frazer wouldn't want you after I had regaled him with the details of your surrender!"

"Oh, you're vile – evil!" she exclaimed, shaking her head from side to side. "Lewis, stop talking like this! We've been friends. Don't destroy everything between us!"

She struggled to free herself, and as her fingers brushed the desk they encountered the solid mass of the paperweight. Her fingers closed over it, and then relaxed again. What did she intend to do with it? Hit him over the head? Oh, that would be too melodramatic! These things just didn't happen any more. Lewis would come to his senses. He was surely trying to frighten her, that was all. Even so, she didn't care for his humour.

Lewis released her suddenly, and she almost fell, clutching the chair weakly to support herself. "Thank goodness," she murmured weakly, and then she realized he was closing the door and turning the key firmly in the lock. "Lewis!" she exclaimed incredulously, but he seemed indifferent to her pleas.

She lifted the paperweight again, and considered hurling at him. But to do so to stop him would require more strength than she possessed and instead she turned and hurled it through the window behind her. There was the hideous sound of crashing glass and then silence.

Lewis was flabbergasted for a moment. "You destructive little fool!" he snarled angrily. "Have you any idea of the cost of a window like that?"

Karen glared at him, trying to hide the fear that was rapidly overtaking her. "You talk to me about destruction!" she cried indignantly. "Haven't you destroyed plenty of things in your time? My marriage, for example."

"You believe that of me?" he cried tormentedly.

Suddenly there was a knocking at the outer door of the office, and Lewis turned frowningly, while Karen felt a surge of relief.

"Martin!" came a familiar voice. "Open this door! I want to speak to you!"

Karen's eyes widened. "Oh, Paul!" she called, in disbelief. "Paul, I'm here!"

The knocking increased, and with resignation Lewis unlocked the door and admitted the other man. Paul's eyes flew from Karen to Lewis and then back to Karen again.

"Are you all right?" he asked, his eyes blazing angrily.

Karen nodded silently, and wrapped her coat closely about her.

"Yes, yes, I'm fine," she said at last, trying to stop her lips from trembling.

Lewis walked to his desk and then turned to face them. Paul studied the older man's face savagely. "If you'd harmed her I think I would have killed you," he bit out violently.

Lewis pale face was flushed. "I never touched her," he denied, coldly. "Now – or ever!"

Paul glanced at Karen, and she swallowed hard. "You – you locked the door," she whispered.

Lewis sneered. "Only to frighten you. I've never raped a woman yet, and I don't intend to start now," he snapped harshly. "Take your little woman, Frazer, and get out of here. I never want to see either of you again."

"Wait outside, Karen," said Paul quietly, and Karen hesitated only a moment before doing as she was told.

She walked along to the lift, and waited impatiently, shivering a little. There were few sounds from the office and she wondered what Paul was saying to him. Then there was a noise like a crack, and a thump, and a few minutes later Paul joined her, putting on his gloves.

She looked questioningly at him and he smiled wryly. "I've just done something I've wanted to do for a very long time," he remarked. "Now, shall we go back to the apartment?"

Karen nodded.

The warmth of the apartment had never seemed more welcoming. A table had been laid for two in the alcove and Karen smiled.

"Oh, Paul," she murmured, "you don't know how good it is to be here with you!"

Paul's fingers tightened on her hand, and she went on: "After – after – well, all that excitement, do you think I could take a shower? I feel all hot and sticky."

Paul smiled. "Okay. You know where it is. I'll get Travers to delay dinner for a few minutes."

"All right."

"You'll find a robe hanging on the bathroom door," added Paul suddenly. "That is, if you need it."

Karen gave him a questioning glance, and then turned away. Did he mean what she thought he meant? Or was Lewis right? He wanted an affair!

Leaving him, she went through the bedroom to the bathroom and stripping off her clothes she stepped under the shower. She allowed the water to cascade over her aching body, loving the cleansing feeling it gave her. It was as though she was washing all traces of Lewis from her mind as well as her body.

Her hair was soaking when she had finished, so she rubbed it thoroughly with the thick bath towel, and after drying herself she put on the white bathrobe she found on the door.

Then she crossed to the mirror and combed her hair into smoothness again. It was still damp and clung against her neck. After slipping her feet into a pair of bath mules she walked back to the lounge.

Paul had removed his jacket and was stretched out on a couch, smoking a cigarette, his head resting against a cushion. He rose abruptly as her entrance and said:

"Sit down. I'll get you a drink."

"Thank you." Karen subsided on to the couch and he crossed to the cocktail cabinet and poured her a whisky, adding only a little soda. He handed her the drink and then she said: "Sit down, Paul. There's something I would like to know. How did you come to be at the office at the crucial moment?"

Paul shrugged his shoulders but remained standing. "I had a telephone call from Ruth when I got back to my apartment earlier in the evening. It was about the time when you were going to meet Martin. She had met him for lunch today and she had realized he was in one hell of a state. To begin with, she had played along with him because she hoped he might be able to persuade you to marry him, and thus distract my attention from you once and for all."

Karen shivered in anticipation. "Your attention?" she questioned. "Paul, are you serious?"

Paul loosened his collar. He looked down at her with passionate eyes and then with a muffled exclamation he pulled her up into his arms.

"The drink ..." she began, as his mouth sought the softness of her neck.

"To hell with the drink," he muttered harshly, and his mouth parted hers passionately. Then his fingers caressed her shoulders, pushing the gown aside and seeking the warmth of her throat. "Karen," he groaned, "I adore you. I never stopped loving you, you believe that, don't you? However much I tried to convince you otherwise. You must marry me again!"

Karen pushed him slightly away from her. "Darling," she breathed, "finish what you were saying about Ruth. I want to know."

Paul sighed. "Well, selfish and spoilt as Ruth undoubtedly is, she's not a fool, and Lewis's manner was so strange she eventually decided she'd better call me and let me know that he had said he intended having things out with you tonight. I was worried, so I decided to come to the offices to meet you. When I arrived and heard glass breaking I dashed up to the top floor. When Lewis opened the door and I saw you standing there looking so shocked and pale, I really could have killed him!"

Karen sighed. "Oh, Paul, I can't help but feel sorry

for him."

"Why?" Paul was relentless. "He did his best to ruin our lives."

"I know. But honestly, Paul, surely you must have doubted that I could have an affair with someone like him?"

Paul frowned. "Maybe I did. But you don't know the whole truth of that affair, I fear. Martin came to see me before the divorce. He told me you and he were lovers and that you wanted a divorce but didn't wish to see me yourself. I had to believe him. He was so adamant, and I had no reason to doubt his word at that time. After all, you made no attempt to see me at all, after the separation ..."

"Lewis told me it would be better not to," she explained, sighing now.

"Yes ... well ... I told him I would need definite proof and he agreed to supply it. He gave me details of a night he would be spending at your flat, and I hired a private detective to make everything official. The detective reported that Martin had indeed stayed at your flat all night and I had to believe him. I was furious, and according to Martin there had been other nights. That was the beginning ..."

Karen swallowed hard. It was hurtful to think of Lewis deliberately ruining their marriage like that. Heartlessly, only thinking of himself.

"He stayed at the flat because he said it was too late to go home after we'd finished working. He said he would sleep on the couch and I agreed it would save him having to go all the way to Hampstead. Paul, that's the truth."

Paul smiled and drew her close. "Oh, I believe you," he said softly. "I can see now how easy it is to be deceived."

"Thank goodness," she whispered. "I never wanted to stay away, you know. If you'd only let me know you wanted me I would have come running."

"And now?"

"That's up to you," she whispered. "Can you bear to have me back?"

Paul's mouth caressed her neck. "I can't bear to let you go," he muttered. "Does that answer your question?"

"Oh, yes," she breathed.

"Are you hungry?" he asked gently.

"Only for you," she replied, sliding her arms round his neck. "You aren't going to send me home, are you? Until we can get a licence?"

"Now what do you think?" he murmured, lifting her bodily into his arms.